PRENTICE HALL
WRITING AND
GRAMMAR

Daily Language Practice
Blackline Masters

Grade Twelve

Boston, Massachusetts,
Upper Saddle River, New Jersey

Pearson Prentice Hall™ is a trademark of Pearson Education, Inc.
Pearson® is a registered trademark of Pearson plc.
Prentice Hall® is a registered trademark of Pearson Education, Inc.

ISBN 0-13-361717-3

1 2 3 4 5 6 7 8 9 10   10 09 08 07 06

Contents

Acknowledgments

Harcourt Brace and Company, and Faber and Faber Ltd.
"The Love Song of J. Alfred Prufrock" from *Collected Poems 1909–1962* by T. S. Eliot, copyright 1936 by Harcourt Brace Jovanovich, Inc.; copyright © 1963, 1964, by T. S. Eliot.

Harvard University Press
Lines from "Success is counted sweetest" by Emily Dickinson, reprinted by permission of the publishers and the Trustees of Amherst College from *The Poems of Emily Dickinson*, Thomas H. Johnson, editor, Cambridge, Mass.: The Belknap Press of Harvard University Press. Copyright © 1951, 1955, 1979, 1983 by the President and Fellows of Harvard College.

Introduction

A Tool for Success

The middle and high school years are a crucial period for the development of students' skills in all of the language arts. As a result, students need programs that provide individual and cooperative practice in reading, writing, speaking, and listening skills.

Prentice Hall's *Daily Language Practice* offers just such a framework for meaningful language arts practice. While focusing on grammar, mechanics, and usage skills, the program provides a fresh point of departure from the tedious, time-consuming drills of the past. Using *Daily Language Practice* for just a few minutes a day helps you provide your students with meaningful routines that ensure continuous progress. In effect, *Daily Language Practice* offers you a full toolbox for developing reading, writing, listening, and speaking skills.

Design and Organization

The basic components of language use—reading, writing, speaking, and listening—cannot be learned in isolation from each other. Rather, students learn best when all the language arts are integrated through authentic activities. Literature provides a natural context for practice in all of the language arts and is a natural springboard for teaching the full array of skills. The *Daily Language Practice* lessons are a logical outgrowth of this concept. Each lesson is tied to some aspect of the literature. Some lessons are keyed to specific literature selections, while others relate to literary genres, authors, themes, cross-curricular topics, or cross-cultural issues.

The literature used for *Daily Language Practice* topics reflects the best of the traditional and the contemporary . . . from time-honored classics to fresh voices. Short stories, drama, nonfiction, poetry, and novels are all incorporated. For example, the *Daily Language Practice* activities for Grades 9–12 include sentences that relate to classics, such as Edgar Allan Poe's "The Cask of Amontillado," Homer's *Odyssey*, and Shakespeare's sonnets, as well as contemporary works, such as D.H. Lawrence's "The Rocking-Horse Winner," John Knowles's *A Separate Peace*, and Barry Lopez's "Children of the Woods." There are exercises that discuss detective stories, Mexican customs and traditions, and the art and music of the Renaissance. What a natural, painless way for students to master the fundamentals of standard written English as they experience the rich literature of our varied culture!

Daily Language Practice lessons are organized in a series of thirty-six weeks. You may wish to start or end each language arts lesson with *Daily Language Practice*, or use the sentences as you work through lessons to integrate writing and grammar skills. The practice provides two sentences or passages a day, five days a week. This format allows you to provide your students with regular practice in language and writing skills. By spending five to ten minutes a day in revision and discussion, students will have a regular opportunity to improve their reading, writing, speaking, and listening skills.

By the way, some students may prefer to work on more than two sentences a day! Feel free to be flexible in your scheduling and to pace and work with the program in ways that are most beneficial to your students.

Making the Most of *Daily Language Practice*

We provide sentences in print and on overhead transparencies to facilitate your giving students a variety of options and presentations. Some of the different ways that you can guide your students through the *Daily Language Practice* include the following:

- Write the two Practice Sentences on the board every day. Students can work independently, in pairs, in small groups, or as a class to write and discuss the problems and corrections.
- Using the transparency, place the sentences on an overhead projector. Arrange students in learning groups to work through the sentences, discuss the problems, and make corrections.
- Dictate the sentences for students to write. Invite volunteers to isolate the errors and explain how to correct them.

As students listen, write, and discuss each sentence, they reinforce their listening, thinking, writing, and speaking skills. The combination of written and oral practice fully taps all learning modalities.

Daily Language Practice and Special Needs Populations

Daily Language Practice helps special needs populations by breaking down grammar, usage, and mechanics to their basic parts. ESL and LEP students are often overwhelmed by the sheer mass of information they must absorb. By providing only two, clear-cut passages a day, you can help your special needs students learn to learn in an effective, focused way.

Advantages and Outcomes

Daily Language Practice benefits all learners. Since the sentences build from simple to complex errors in each grade level, students gain confidence as they gain mastery. As they build to more complex skills, such as parallel structure and pronoun agreement, students gain a deeper understanding of the logic behind English structure. By the end of the thirty-six weeks of practice, students will have explored all the common errors in grammar, usage, and mechanics, and will have been presented with the knowledge they need to correct them.

Daily Language Practice

Daily Language Practice • Week 1

Day 1

Skills Practiced

Capitalization of name
of race

Elimination of split infinitive

Use of past perfect tense

Practice Sentences

1. In the A.D. 400's and 500's, three Germanic tribes—the Angles, the Saxons, and the jutes—settled in England.

2. These newcomers began to slowly drive out the native Britons, and by A.D. 600 they occupied nearly all of England.

Answers

1. In the A.D. 400's and 500's, three Germanic tribes—the Angles, the Saxons, and the Jutes—settled in England.

2. These newcomers slowly began to drive out the native Britons, and by A.D. 600 they had occupied nearly all of England.

Day 2

Skills Practiced

Hyphenation of compound
word

Correct relative pronoun

Correct use of *between/among*

Correction of commonly
confused words

Subject and verb agreement

Practice Sentences

1. In England, the Anglo Saxons established seven main kingdoms, who often fought between themselves.

2. Used to war and hardship, Anglo Saxons excepted the belief that everything were controlled by fate.

Answers

1. In England, the Anglo-Saxons established seven main kingdoms, which often fought among themselves.

2. Used to war and hardship, Anglo-Saxons accepted the belief that everything was controlled by fate.

Day 3

Skills Practiced

Elimination of double subject

Correct past participle of irregular verb

Correction of dangling modifier

Use of active voice to improve style

Practice Sentences

1. By the A.D. 600's, Roman missionaries they had arrived and began to convert the Anglo-Saxon kings to Christianity.

2. Promoting peace among warring leaders, the Anglo-Saxon kingdoms were united by the new religion.

Answers

1. By the A.D. 600's, Roman missionaries had arrived and begun to convert the Anglo-Saxon kings to Christianity.

2. Promoting peace among warring leaders, the new religion unified the Anglo-Saxon kingdoms.

Day 4

Skills Practiced

Use of commas in a series

Use of separate sentences to correct run-on sentence

Correction of sentence fragment

Correct placement of period with quotation marks

Practice Sentences

1. Anglo-Saxon literature consisted mainly of spoken poems songs and chants, it was a way to pass on history to illiterate people.

2. All important prose written in Latin because Anglo-Saxon was considered a "vulgar tongue".

Answers

1. Anglo-Saxon literature consisted mainly of spoken poems, songs, and chants. It was a way to pass on history to illiterate people.

2. All important prose was written in Latin because Anglo-Saxon was considered a "vulgar tongue."

Day 5

Skills Practiced

Use of comma after introductory subordinate clause

Correction of unclear pronoun reference

Spelling out number at the beginning of a sentence

Correction of commonly confused words

Practice Sentences

1. After invaders from Denmark and Normandy defeated Anglo-Saxon England it evolved into Middle English.

2. 20 percent of the words in English and much of it's grammar come from Anglo-Saxon.

Answers

1. After invaders from Denmark and Normandy defeated Anglo-Saxon England, the language evolved into Middle English.

2. Twenty percent of the words in English and much of its grammar come from Anglo-Saxon.

Daily Language Practice • Week 2

Day 1

Skills Practiced

Elimination of double comparison

Use of underlining or italics with title of long literary work

Correct relative pronoun

Practice Sentences

1. No Anglo-Saxon poem is more better known than Beowulf, the story of a warrior.

2. Composed by an unknown poet that lived 1,200 years ago, this epic marks the beginning of English literature.

Answers

1. No Anglo-Saxon poem is better known than <u>Beowulf</u>, the story of a warrior.

2. Composed by an unknown poet who lived 1,200 years ago, this epic marks the beginning of English literature.

Day 2

Skills Practiced

Correct superlative form of adjective

Use of colon before a list

Correct pronoun case

Use of commas with coordinate adjectives

Practice Sentences

1. The warrior Beowulf embodies the most high ideals of his time, loyalty, bravery, and selflessness.

2. Him and his followers sail to Denmark to defeat the fierce bloodthirsty monster Grendel.

Answers

1. The warrior Beowulf embodies the highest ideals of his time: loyalty, bravery, and selflessness.

2. He and his followers sail to Denmark to defeat the fierce, bloodthirsty monster Grendel.

Day 3

Skills Practiced

Use of comma before coordinating conjunction in a compound sentence

Correction of commonly confused words

Use of subordinating conjunction *so that*

Use of specific noun to improve style

Practice Sentences

1. <u>Beowulf</u> was composed about A.D. 700 but three centuries had past before it was first written down.

2. Anglo-Saxon singers memorized all 3,000 lines so they could recite the thing to audiences.

Answers

1. <u>Beowulf</u> was composed about A.D. 700, but three centuries had passed before it was first written down.

2. Anglo-Saxon singers memorized all 3,000 lines so that they could recite the epic poem to audiences.

Day 4

Skills Practiced

Use of comma with absolute phrase

Correction of commonly confused words

Use of commas with nonrestrictive participial phrase

Correct past form of irregular verb

Practice Sentences

1. Sword ready Beowulf was laying in wait for the monster Grendel.

2. Grendel's mother filled with rage seeked revenge for the death of her son.

Answers

1. Sword ready, Beowulf was lying in wait for the monster Grendel.

2. Grendel's mother, filled with rage, sought revenge for the death of her son.

Day 5

Skills Practiced

Use of periods with initials

Correct capitalization in titles

Correct spelling of plural form

Use of hyphen with suffix *like*

Practice Sentences

1. The poetry of <u>Beowulf</u> inspired J R R Tolkien, an Oxford scholar, to write <u>The Hobbit</u> and <u>The Lord Of The Rings</u>.

2. In these and other best-selling novels, Tolkien shows brave heros struggling against Grendel like monsters.

Answers

1. The poetry of <u>Beowulf</u> inspired J. R. R. Tolkien, an Oxford scholar, to write <u>The Hobbit</u> and <u>The Lord of the Rings</u>.

2. In these and other best-selling novels, Tolkien shows brave heroes struggling against Grendel-like monsters.

Daily Language Practice • Week 3

Day 1

Skills Practiced

Use of 's to form singular possessive

Pronoun agreement with antecedent

Capitalization of proper adjectives

Use of semicolon to correct run-on sentence

Practice Sentences

1. A culture or societies highest values are exemplified by their heroes.

2. In greek and roman myths, heroes are often the children of gods they usually have some supernatural abilities.

Answers

1. A culture or society's highest values are exemplified by its heroes.

2. In Greek and Roman myths, heroes are often the children of gods; they usually have some supernatural abilities.

Day 2

Skills Practiced

Elimination of faulty parallel structure

Correct indefinite article

Elimination of double negative

Use of commas in series

Practice Sentences

1. The true hero ventures into the unknown to answer a question, solve a problem, or for reaching a important goal.

2. Hardly no heroic quest is complete without danger suffering or trials.

Answers

1. The true hero ventures into the unknown to answer a question, solve a problem, or reach an important goal.

2. Hardly any heroic quest is complete without danger, suffering, or trials.

Day 3

Skills Practiced

Elimination of passive voice

Elimination of *and* at the beginning of sentence

Correction of commonly misused words

Practice Sentences

1. In an epic, fabulous forces are encountered by a hero, and a decisive victory is won.

2. And returning from the mysterious adventure, the hero takes special gifts or knowledge to his people.

Answers

1. In an epic, a hero encounters fabulous forces and wins a decisive victory.

2. Returning from the mysterious adventure, the hero brings special gifts or knowledge to his people.

Day 4

Skills Practiced

Capitalization of name of region

Use of adverb to modify verb

Use of underlining or italics with movie title

Practice Sentences

1. For much of this century, the sheriffs of the old west accommodated our need for heroes.

2. More recent, Luke Skywalker of Star Wars fame became a hero to millions.

Answers

1. For much of this century, the sheriffs of the Old West accommodated our need for heroes.

2. More recently, Luke Skywalker of <u>Star Wars</u> fame became a hero to millions.

Day 5

Skills Practiced

Correction of commonly confused words

Correct past participle of irregular verb

Use of comma in series

Practice Sentences

1. You're favorite action film stars act like traditional heroes in many ways.

2. Have they showed strength courage nobility and leadership in their successful quests?

Answers

1. Your favorite action film stars act like traditional heroes in many ways.

2. Have they shown strength, courage, nobility, and leadership in their successful quests?

Daily Language Practice • Week 4

Day 1

Skills Practiced

- Correct use of relative pronoun in a restrictive clause
- Correct coordinating conjunction
- Correct superlative form of adjective

Practice Sentences

1. Ballads are anonymous narrative songs, which have been preserved orally.
2. Any culture can produce ballads, and they are commonest in primitive societies.

Answers

1. Ballads are anonymous narrative songs that have been preserved orally.
2. Any culture can produce ballads, but they are most common in primitive societies.

Day 2

Skills Practiced

- Use of hyphen with compound adjective
- Elimination of *here* after a demonstrative adjective
- Use of separate sentences to correct run-on sentence

Practice Sentences

1. Between 1200 and 1700, many fine ballads were composed along the English Scottish border.
2. Were these here ballads written by a single poet or as a group effort, no one knows for sure.

Answers

1. Between 1200 and 1700, many fine ballads were composed along the English-Scottish border.
2. Were these ballads written by a single poet or as a group effort? No one knows for sure.

Day 3

Skills Practiced

- Elimination of double comparison
- Use of quotation marks with titles of poems
- Use of active voice to improve style

Practice Sentences

1. The more better-known ballads, such as <u>Sir Patrick Spens</u> and <u>Barbara Allan</u>, usually deal with death or murder.
2. Many different versions were developed by balladeers.

Answers

1. The better-known ballads, such as "Sir Patrick Spens" and "Barbara Allan," usually deal with death or murder.
2. Balladeers developed many different versions.

Day 4

Skills Practiced

Correct past participle of irregular verb

Correction of commonly confused words

Use of commas to set off appositive

Correction of commonly misspelled word

Practice Sentences

1. Since ballads were originally sang to simple tunes, there narrative structure is quite straightforward.

2. Another aspect of choral music, the refrain accounts for the prevelence of repetition in many ballads.

Answers

1. Since ballads were originally sung to simple tunes, their narrative structure is quite straightforward.

2. Another aspect of choral music, the refrain, accounts for the prevalence of repetition in many ballads.

Day 5

Skills Practiced

Correct coordinating conjunction

Use of end punctuation: question mark

Subject and verb agreement

Elimination of unnecessary preposition

Practice Sentences

1. Are you familiar with American ballads that recount the lives and deaths of Casey Jones, John Henry, or Jesse James.

2. Johnny Cash is one of our modern singers who carries on the tradition of singing ballads.

Answers

1. Are you familiar with American ballads that recount the lives and deaths of Casey Jones, John Henry, and Jesse James?

2. Johnny Cash is one of our modern singers who carry on with the tradition of singing ballads.

Daily Language Practice • Week 5

Day 1

Skills Practiced

- Correction of commonly misspelled word
- Correct use of dash to emphasize additional information
- Subject and verb agreement
- Elimination of double negatives

Practice Sentences

1. For midevil artists of Europe, the Christian religion—not people or nature, was the chief subject matter.
2. There weren't but one area in which to exhibit their work—cathedrals or churches.

Answers

1. For medieval artists of Europe, the Christian religion—not people or nature—was the chief subject matter.
2. There was only one area in which to exhibit their work—cathedrals or churches.

Day 2

Skills Practiced

- Capitalization of religious terms
- Use of adverb to modify adjective
- Correct subordinating conjunction

Practice Sentences

1. Colorful illustrations for bibles had abstract patterns of elaborate arranged lines.
2. Decorated with gold, the manuscripts were called illuminations because they looked like they had been lit up.

Answers

1. Colorful illustrations for Bibles had abstract patterns of elaborately arranged lines.
2. Decorated with gold, the manuscripts were called illuminations because they looked as if they had been lit up.

Day 3

Skills Practiced

- Capitalization of proper adjective
- Correct placement of period with parentheses
- Use of hyphen with compound adjective

Practice Sentences

1. A style of art called byzantine art arose in Byzantium (now Istanbul, Turkey.)
2. In this style, much unchanged to the present day, figures stand for religious ideas, not flesh and blood people.

Answers

1. A style of art called Byzantine art arose in Byzantium (now Istanbul, Turkey).
2. In this style, much unchanged to the present day, figures stand for religious ideas, not flesh-and-blood people.

Day 4

Skills Practiced

Subject and verb agreement

Correct predicate adjective

Use of comma before coordinating conjunction

Verb tense compatibility

Practice Sentences

1. Colorful Romanesque art look well on the stone walls of churches.

2. Romanesque paintings lack perspective but they showed skill in composition.

Answers

1. Colorful Romanesque art looks good on the stone walls of churches.

2. Romanesque paintings lack perspective, but they show skill in composition.

Day 5

Skills Practiced

Correction of faulty subordination

Use of hyphen in compound adjective

Use of commas with nonrestrictive participial phrase

Correction of commonly confused words

Practice Sentences

1. Gothic architecture featured giant windows because artists filled them with beautiful stained glass scenes.

2. Armies of sculptors working anonymously decorated the great churches farther with carvings and statues.

Answers

1. Because Gothic architecture featured giant windows, artists filled them with beautiful stained-glass scenes.

2. Armies of sculptors, working anonymously, decorated the great churches further with carvings and statues.

Daily Language Practice • Week 6

Day 1

Skills Practiced

Subject and verb agreement

Correction of unclear pronoun reference

Correction of commonly confused words

Practice Sentences

1. Written in the late 1300's, <u>The Canterbury Tales</u> rank as one of your finest works of literature.

2. Among England's greatest poets, Geoffrey Chaucer stands besides William Shakespeare and John Milton.

Answers

1. Written in the late 1300's, <u>The Canterbury Tales</u> ranks as one of the world's finest works of literature.

2. Among England's greatest poets, Geoffrey Chaucer stands beside William Shakespeare and John Milton.

Day 2

Skills Practiced

Spelling out numbers through one hundred

Correct use of *fewer* and *less*

Use of comma to separate parts of an address

Subject and verb agreement

Practice Sentences

1. The 24 tales, about 100 less than Chaucer planned, tell of pilgrims on their way to Canterbury England.

2. Each of the pilgrims, who come from society's different classes, tell a tale.

Answers

1. The twenty-four tales, about one hundred fewer than Chaucer planned, tell of pilgrims on their way to Canterbury, England.

2. Each of the pilgrims, who come from society's different classes, tells a tale.

Day 3

Skills Practiced

Use of hyphen with prefix *self-*

Correct use of past perfect tense

Verb tense compatibility

Correct use of helping verb *have*

Correct spelling of homophones

Practice Sentences

1. Largely selfeducated, Chaucer served as a soldier before he become the king's special counselor.

2. His wide travels would of lead him to see all classes of society firsthand.

Answers

1. Largely self-educated, Chaucer had served as a soldier before he became the king's special counselor.

2. His wide travels would have led him to see all classes of society firsthand.

	Skills Practiced	**Practice Sentences**
Day 4	Correct use of absolute adjective Capitalization of first word in title Use of precise adjectives to improve style Pronoun agreement with antecedent	1. Characterization is the most perfect part of <u>the Canterbury Tales</u>. 2. Using interesting details, Chaucer draws nice portraits of their characters. **Answers** 1. Characterization is the perfect part of <u>The Canterbury Tales</u>. 2. Using interesting details, Chaucer draws shrewd and affectionate portraits of his characters.

	Skills Practiced	**Practice Sentences**
Day 5	Elimination of split infinitive Capitalization of name of a language Use of adverb to modify adjective	1. To fully appreciate Chaucer's rich language and rhymed couplets, you have to read the original middle english. 2. Because this language is real difficult, almost everyone reads modern translations of the tales. **Answers** 1. To appreciate Chaucer's rich language and rhymed couplets fully, you have to read the original Middle English. 2. Because this language is really difficult, almost everyone reads modern translations of the tales.

Daily Language Practice • Week 7

Day 1

Skills Practiced

Correct formation of irregular verb tense

Correction of misplaced modifier

Use of italics or underlining with foreign words

Correct relative pronoun

Use of comma with non-restrictive clause

Practice Sentences

1. The Renaissance was a great cultural movement that begun in Italy in the early 1300's, lasting some 200 years.

2. The name comes from the Latin word rinascere that means "to be reborn."

Answers

1. The Renaissance, lasting some 200 years, was a great cultural movement that began in Italy in the early 1300's.

2. The name comes from the Latin word rinascere, which means "to be reborn."

Day 2

Skills Practiced

Elimination of redundancy

Subject and verb agreement

Use of comma after introductory phrase

Practice Sentences

1. The goal of capturing the spirit of ancient Greek and Roman cultures were the aim of Renaissance artists and thinkers.

2. Unlike medieval thinkers who viewed society as evil the Renaissance thinkers saw it as a civilizing force.

Answers

1. Capturing the spirit of ancient Greek and Roman cultures was the aim of Renaissance artists and thinkers.

2. Unlike medieval thinkers who viewed society as evil, Renaissance thinkers saw it as a civilizing force.

Day 3

Skills Practiced

Subject and verb agreement

Capitalization of name of historical period

Elimination of dangling modifier

Use of comma with coordinate adjectives

Practice Sentences

1. The majesty of the human mind and body were important themes of the renaissance.

2. Unlike the stiff figures of medieval religious art, Renaissance artists painted natural lifelike figures.

Answers

1. The majesty of the human mind and body was an important theme of the Renaissance.

2. Renaissance artists painted natural, lifelike figures unlike the stiff figures of medieval religious art.

---

18 Daily Language Practice

Day 4

Skills Practiced

Use of active voice to improve style

Use of colon before a list

Elimination of faulty parallel structure

Correction of commonly confused words

Practice Sentences

1. Renaissance art was dominated by three artists, Michelangelo, Raphael, and Leonardo da Vinci.

2. Because he was an artist, an engineer, and performed science experiments, da Vinci typifies the "Renaissance man"—a person who's interests know no bounds.

Answers

1. Three artists dominated Renaissance art: Michelangelo, Raphael, and Leonardo da Vinci.

2. Because he was an artist, an engineer, and a scientist, da Vinci typifies the "Renaissance man"—a person whose interests know no bounds.

Day 5

Skills Practiced

Correct spelling of homophones

Correct use of capitalization in name of school courses

Use of commas to set off appositive

Verb tense compatibility

Practice Sentences

1. Renaissance ideas lead universities to offer humanities courses, such as History and Poetry for the first time.

2. Independent thinkers debated religion and morality, and some were even questioning the teachings of the Church.

Answers

1. Renaissance ideas led universities to offer humanities courses, such as history and poetry, for the first time.

2. Independent thinkers debated religion and morality, and some even questioned the teachings of the Church.

Daily Language Practice • Week 8

Day 1

Skills Practiced

Capitalization of adjective formed from name of geographic area

Use of colon to introduce illustrative material

Capitalization of title before a person's name

Elimination of redundancy

Practice Sentences

1. The Faust legend illustrates a common theme in western literature the urge to go beyond normal limits of human power.

2. In the original legend, doctor John Faustus sold his soul to the devil in order for to get knowledge of magic.

Answers

1. The Faust legend illustrates a common theme in Western literature: the urge to go beyond normal limits of human power.

2. In the original legend, Doctor John Faustus sold his soul to the devil to get knowledge of magic.

Day 2

Skills Practiced

Pronoun/antecedent agreement

Correction of misplaced phrase

Correction of sentence fragment

Correct use of helping verb *have*

Practice Sentences

1. Faust is a Renaissance hero whose aim is to realize their full potential at any cost in Christopher Marlowe's play.

2. Faust's desire for knowledge in conflict with the medieval view that salvation should of been his main concern.

Answers

1. In Christopher Marlowe's play, Faust is a Renaissance hero whose aim is to realize his full potential at any cost.

2. Faust's desire for knowledge was in conflict with the medieval view that salvation should have been his main concern.

Day 3

Skills Practiced

Correct past form of irregular verb

Use of active voice to improve style

Elimination of faulty parallel structure

Practice Sentences

1. Marlowe drew inspiration from the classics and brang Renaissance learning to his plays.

2. His plays, in which great learning was blended with deep emotion, show zest for life, not coldly formal.

Answers

1. Marlowe drew inspiration from the classics and brought Renaissance learning to his plays.

2. His plays, which blend great learning with deep emotion, show zest for life, not a cold formality.

Day 4

Skills Practiced

Correct use of *between* and *among*

Correction of commonly misspelled word

Use of adverb to modify verb

Correction of commonly confused words

Practice Sentences

1. Doctor Faustus's mind is torn among the desire for worldly knowledge and the conciousness of human limitations.

2. This is sure a tragedy that retains it's power and meaning for modern audiences.

Answers

1. Doctor Faustus's mind is torn between the desire for worldly knowledge and the consciousness of human limitations.

2. This is surely a tragedy that retains its power and meaning for modern audiences.

Day 5

Skills Practiced

Use of commas with nonrestrictive clause

Use of comma to set off appositive

Correction of commonly misspelled word

Practice Sentences

1. In his own life about which little is known Christopher Marlowe mirrors his tragic hero.

2. A freethinker he reached great heights in drama only to be asassinated in his twenties for his political views.

Answers

1. In his own life, about which little is known, Christopher Marlowe mirrors his tragic hero.

2. A freethinker, he reached great heights in drama only to be assassinated in his twenties for his political views.

Daily Language Practice • Week 9

Day 1

Skills Practiced

Elimination of redundancy

Use of quotation marks to show a writer's exact words

Use of comma with coordinating conjunction

Correction of vague pronoun reference

Correction of sentence fragment

Practice Sentences

1. Writing of William Shakespeare (1564–1616) Ben Jonson once wrote, He was not of an age, but for all time!

2. The words were prophetic for he is still performed throughout the world. The most beloved English poet of all.

Answers

1. Of William Shakespeare (1564–1616) Ben Jonson once wrote, "He was not of an age, but for all time!"

2. The words were prophetic, for Shakespeare's plays are still performed throughout the world. He remains the most beloved English poet.

Day 2

Skills Practiced

Correct indefinite article

Subject and verb agreement

Correct case of relative pronoun

Revision of sentence ending with preposition

Practice Sentences

1. Among English authors in the 1500's, a autobiographical sequence of sonnets were a fashionable literary form.

2. Scholars have long debated the identities of the young nobleman and lady who Shakespeare dedicated his 154 sonnets to.

Answers

1. Among English authors in the 1500's, an autobiographical sequence of sonnets was a fashionable literary form.

2. Scholars have long debated the identities of the young nobleman and lady to whom Shakespeare dedicated his 154 sonnets.

Day 3

Skills Practiced

Spelling out numbers through one hundred

Use of commas to set off an appositive

Revision of wordy sentence

Practice Sentences

1. A Shakespearean sonnet, 14 lines in iambic pentameter consists of 3 quatrains and a rhyming couplet.

2. What these sonnets usually do is present a problem in the quatrains and offer a solution in the couplet.

Answers

1. A Shakespearean sonnet, fourteen lines in iambic pentameter, consists of three quatrains and a rhyming couplet.

2. These sonnets usually present a problem in the quatrains and offer a solution in the couplet.

Day 4

Skills Practiced

Elimination of double negative

Correction of unclear pronoun reference

Elimination of faulty parallel structure

Correct superlative form of adjective

Practice Sentences

1. Shakespeare's sonnets don't have no titles, so they refer to them by their first line or by the number assigned to them.

2. The destructive effects of time, the quickness of physical decay, and losing love are the commonest themes.

Answers

1. Shakespeare's sonnets have no titles, so readers refer to them by their first line or by the number assigned to them.

2. The destructive effects of time, the quickness of physical decay, and the loss of love are the most common themes.

Day 5

Skills Practiced

Correction of commonly misspelled word

Use of comma after introductory subordinate clause

Use of colon to introduce a clarifying idea

Use of specific noun to improve style

Use of underlining or italics with title of play

Practice Sentences

1. Although the playright wrote the sonnets over a period of several years in the late 1590's they were published in 1609.

2. One thing is sure, these sonnets are clearly from the same man who produced Hamlet, Macbeth, and Romeo and Juliet.

Answers

1. Although the playwright wrote the sonnets over a period of several years in the late 1590's, they were published in 1609.

2. One thing is sure: these sonnets are clearly from the same genius who produced <u>Hamlet</u>, <u>Macbeth</u>, and <u>Romeo and Juliet</u>.

Daily Language Practice • Week 10

Day 1

Skills Practiced

Revision to clarify pronoun reference

Spelling out ordinal numbers

Correct spelling of plural

Practice Sentences

1. Basing it loosely on actual historical events and figures, Shakespeare completed <u>Macbeth</u> in 1606.

2. The setting is Scotland in the 10th and 11th centurys, when King James's family, the Stuarts, first came to the throne.

Answers

1. Shakespeare completed <u>Macbeth</u> in 1606, basing it loosely on actual historical events and figures.

2. The setting is Scotland in the tenth and eleventh centuries, when King James's family, the Stuarts, first came to the throne.

Day 2

Skills Practiced

Elimination of faulty parallel structure

Correction of unclear pronoun reference

Correct comparative form of adjective

Revision of stringy sentence

Practice Sentences

1. Macbeth is brave and has nobility, but they are offset by his overwhelming ambition.

2. Lady Macbeth's ambition is no littler than her husband's, and she is hard, and she lacks his subtle awareness.

Answers

1. Macbeth is brave and noble, but these traits are offset by his overwhelming ambition.

2. Lady Macbeth's ambition is no less than her husband's; however, she is harder and lacks his subtle awareness.

Day 3

Skills Practiced

Formation of plural possessive

Use of commas in a series

Subject and verb agreement

Use of subordinate clause to combine sentences

Practice Sentences

1. In <u>Macbeth</u>, the witches predictions the murders and the sleepwalking create a mood of foreboding.

2. The images of blood and darkness proliferates. The horror intensifies.

Answers

1. In <u>Macbeth</u>, the witches' predictions, the murders, and the sleepwalking create a mood of foreboding.

2. As the images of blood and darkness proliferate, the horror intensifies.

Day 4

Skills Practiced

Correction of faulty subordination

Subject and verb agreement

Correct pronoun case

Correction of commonly misspelled word

Practice Sentences

1. Because he becomes involved in a series of events that lead to his downfall, Macbeth has a tragic flaw.

2. In their attempt to seize the throne, him and his wife ignore their conscences.

Answers

1. Because Macbeth has a tragic flaw, he becomes involved in a series of events that leads to his downfall.

2. In their attempt to seize the throne, he and his wife ignore their consciences.

Day 5

Skills Practiced

Correction of commonly confused words

Use of semicolon to correct run-on sentence

Verb tense compatibility

Use of ellipsis points in a partial quotation

Practice Sentence

1. Macbeth gives in to his evil impulses and looses all emotion, in the end he can't even respond to his wife's death.

2. He concludes that life was only "a tale . . . signifying nothing."

Answer

1. Macbeth gives in to his evil impulses and loses all emotion; in the end he can't even respond to his wife's death.

2. He concludes that life is only "a tale . . . signifying nothing."

Daily Language Practice • Week 11

Day 1

Skills Practiced

- Capitalization of names of religious terms
- Use of commas with nonrestrictive clause
- Correction of commonly confused words

Practice Sentences

1. The bible, which is divided into the Old Testament and the New Testament is a sacred book.
2. The Jewish religion excepts only the Old Testament, while the Christian religion excepts the Old Testament and the New Testament.

Answers

1. The Bible, which is divided into the Old Testament and the New Testament, is a sacred book.
2. The Jewish religion accepts only the Old Testament, while the Christian religion accepts the Old Testament and the New Testament.

Day 2

Skills Practiced

- Correction of misplaced modifier
- Use of periods with abbreviations
- Verb tense compatibility
- Correct placement of B.C./A.D.

Practice Sentences

1. The Old Testament from about 1300 BC to 100 BC deals largely with the history and religious life of ancient Israel.
2. The New Testament began with the birth of Jesus Christ and covers about 100 years, ending about 125 AD.

Answers

1. The Old Testament deals largely with the history and religious life of ancient Israel from about 1300 B.C. to 100 B.C.
2. The New Testament begins with the birth of Jesus Christ and covers about 100 years, ending about A.D. 125.

Day 3

Skills Practiced

- Correct use of *fewer* and *less*
- Revision of wordy sentence
- Elimination of unnecessary hyphen in a compound modifier
- Use of exclamation point to show strong emotion

Practice Sentences

1. No less than a dozen English translations of the Bible preceded the King James Version, a version that was first published in 1611.
2. How great, indeed, was the impact on English prose and poetry of this widely-read masterpiece.

Answers

1. No fewer than a dozen English translations of the Bible preceded the King James Version, first published in 1611.
2. How great, indeed, was the impact on English prose and poetry of this widely read masterpiece!

Day 4

Skills Practiced

- Correction of commonly misspelled word
- Use of commas in a series
- Correction of commonly confused words
- Elimination of faulty parallel structure

Practice Sentences

1. The Talmud, the acumulated and authoritative body of Jewish oral traditions, includes sections dealing with law folklore and domestic life.
2. It's main divisions are the Mishna, a text of the oral law, and the Gemara, which interprets the Mishna.

Answers

1. The Talmud, the accumulated and authoritative body of Jewish oral traditions, includes sections dealing with law, folklore, and domestic life.
2. Its main divisions are the Mishna, a text of the oral law, and the Gemara, an interpretation of the Mishna.

Day 5

Skills Practiced

- Correction of commonly confused words
- Correct spelling: doubling final consonant
- Use of numerals above one hundred
- Use of underlining or italics with foreign word

Practice Sentences

1. Muslims believe that there sacred book, the Koran, was revealed to Muhammad by an angel beginning about A.D. 610.
2. This text was written in rhymed Arabic and divided into a hundred and fourteen chapters, called suras.

Answers

1. Muslims believe that their sacred book, the Koran, was revealed to Muhammad by an angel beginning about A.D. 610.
2. This text was written in rhymed Arabic and divided into 114 chapters, called <u>suras</u>.

Daily Language Practice • Week 12

Day 1

Skills Practiced

Capitalization of title before person's name

Correct pronoun case

Correct use of relative pronoun

Elimination of commas with restrictive clause

Capitalization of religious terms

Use of commas with appositive

Practice Sentences

1. In 1534, king Henry VIII had Parliament pass a law saying that him, not the pope, was head of the English Church.

2. Henry's action led to the formation of a church, which had more in common with calvinist, or puritan Protestantism.

Answers

1. In 1534, King Henry VIII had Parliament pass a law saying that he, not the pope, was head of the English Church.

2. Henry's action led to the formation of a church that had more in common with Calvinist, or Puritan, Protestantism.

Day 2

Skills Practiced

Use of comma after introductory prepositional phrases

Correction of sentence fragment

Correct use of *between* and *among*

Correction of faulty subordinate clause

Practice Sentence

1. During the long reign of Queen Elizabeth I the English Church holding a middle course among Roman Catholicism and Puritanism.

2. Elizabeth's cousin, James VI, took the throne in 1603 when he made no secret of his dislike for Puritans.

Answers

1. During the long reign of Queen Elizabeth I, the English Church held a middle course between Roman Catholicism and Puritanism.

2. When Elizabeth's cousin, James VI, took the throne in 1603, he made no secret of his dislike for Puritans.

Day 3

Skills Practiced

- Correct comparative form
- Correct formation of possessive
- Correct spelling: *ie/ei*
- Correct past form of irregular verb

Practice Sentences

1. Religious tension grew worser under James son, Charles I, who tried to force the Puritans to conform to his views.
2. In 1642, when Charles tried to sieze Puritans in Parliament who had called him a tyrant, the Civil War begun.

Answers

1. Religious tension grew worse under James's son, Charles I, who tried to force the Puritans to conform to his views.
2. In 1642, when Charles tried to seize Puritans in Parliament who had called him a tyrant, the Civil War began.

Day 4

Skills Practiced

- Elimination of faulty parallel structure
- Spelling out numbers through one hundred
- Elimination of double negative

Practice Sentences

1. Under Oliver Cromwell the Puritans defeated Charles's armies, trying the king, and eventually had him beheaded.
2. For 10 years, Cromwell and Parliament ruled without no monarch, but the English soon tired of the strict Puritan rule.

Answers

1. Under Oliver Cromwell the Puritans defeated Charles's armies, tried the king, and eventually had him beheaded.
2. For ten years, Cromwell and Parliament ruled without a monarch, but the English soon tired of the strict Puritan rule.

Day 5

Skills Practiced

- Use of commas to set off appositive
- Elimination of *but* at beginning of sentence
- Use of subordinating conjunction to combine sentences
- Use of hyphens in compound noun

Practice Sentences

1. The monarchy was restored in 1660, and the late king's sons, Charles II and James II a Roman Catholic, sat on the throne until 1688.
2. But the old religious tensions flared, and James II fled to France. His Protestant daughter and son in law, Mary and William III, became monarchs.

Answers

1. The monarchy was restored in 1660, and the late king's sons, Charles II and James II, a Roman Catholic, sat on the throne until 1688.
2. When the old religious tensions flared, James II fled to France, and his Protestant daughter and son-in-law, Mary and William III, became monarchs.

Daily Language Practice • Week 13

Day 1

Skills Practiced

Correct use of absolute adjective

Correct past participle of irregular verb

Correction of unclear pronoun reference

Practice Sentences

1. John Donne is the most supreme example of the metaphysical poets, a name commonly gave to a group of English poets in the 1600's.

2. Inspired by philosophical views of the universe, they examined the role of the human spirit in the drama of life.

Answers

1. John Donne is the supreme example of the metaphysical poets, a name commonly given to a group of English poets in the 1600's.

2. Inspired by philosophical views of the universe, these poets examined the role of the human spirit in the drama of life.

Day 2

Skills Practiced

Use of semicolon to correct run-on sentence

Elimination of faulty parallel structure

Elimination of redundancy

Practice Sentences

1. As a young man, Donne delighted in the composition of love poems, religious poetry was the interest he turned to in later life.

2. In both, Donne showed the same exact intensity and wit, using elaborate and fanciful comparisons called conceits.

Answers

1. As a young man, Donne delighted in the composition of love poems; he turned to religious poetry in later life.

2. In both, Donne showed the same intensity and wit, using elaborate and fanciful comparisons called conceits.

Day 3	**Skills Practiced** Use of quotation marks to show a writer's exact words Correct use of ellipsis points for partial quotation Correct placement of period with quotation marks	**Practice Sentences** 1. Everyone is familiar with Donne's unforgettable words No man is an island, entire of itself.... 2. In the same paragraph, Donne writes, "....never send to know for whom the bell tolls; it tolls for thee". **Answers** 1. Everyone is familiar with Donne's unforgettable words, "No man is an island, entire of itself..." 2. In the same paragraph, Donne writes, "...never send to know for whom the bell tolls; it tolls for thee."
Day 4	**Skills Practiced** Correction of dangling modifier Capitalization of religious terms Use of commas to set off appositive	**Practice Sentence** 1. A master at blending thought and emotion, Donne's forceful language has the quality of everyday speech. 2. In his forties, John Donne became an anglican priest, and his sermons, magnificent performances attracted huge crowds. **Answers** 1. A master at blending thought and emotion, Donne used forceful language with the quality of everyday speech. 2. In his forties, John Donne became an Anglican priest, and his sermons, magnificent performances, attracted huge crowds.
Day 5	**Skills Practiced** Elimination of unnecessary hyphen Use of adverbs to modify verbs Correction of unclear pronoun reference	**Practice Sentences** 1. Largely ignored for almost 300 years, the work of John Donne was re-discovered in this century. 2. Doubtless, Donne's internal conflict between hope and disillusionment speaks as sincere to our age as it did theirs. **Answers** 1. Largely ignored for almost 300 years, the work of John Donne was rediscovered in this century. 2. Doubtlessly, Donne's internal conflict between hope and disillusionment speaks as sincerely to our age as it did the poet's.

Daily Language Practice • Week 14

Day 1

Skills Practiced

- Elimination of commas with restrictive appositive
- Use of quotation marks to call attention to words or phrases
- Use of hyphen with compound modifier

Practice Sentences

1. A favorite in the court of King James I, the poet and playwright, Ben Jonson, exercised great influence over English literature.
2. The young writers who flocked to Jonson, calling themselves the Sons of Ben, included the century's best known poets.

Answers

1. A favorite in the court of King James I, the poet and playwright Ben Jonson exercised great influence over English literature.
2. The young writers who flocked to Jonson, calling themselves the "Sons of Ben," included the century's best-known poets.

Day 2

Skills Practiced

- Use of hyphen with prefix *all-*
- Correct use of dashes to set off explanatory information
- Use of quotation marks to show speaker's exact words

Practice Sentences

1. For the all important royal court, Jonson prepared masques—elaborate shows that included his best poems, as well as song, dance, and allegorical stories.
2. His deceptively simple poems were the result of hard work; of "Song: To Celia," he claimed that he had sweated it into shape.

Answers

1. For the all-important royal court, Jonson prepared masques—elaborate shows that included his best poems—as well as song, dance, and allegorical stories.
2. His deceptively simple poems were the result of hard work; of "Song: To Celia," he claimed that he had "sweated it into shape."

Day 3

Skills Practiced

- Revision of choppy sentences
- Use of commas with nonrestrictive clause
- Pronoun agreement with antecedent
- Elimination of unnecessary comma with restrictive clause

Practice Sentences

1. Robert Herrick was a minister. He was influenced by Ben Jonson. He took England's lush countryside as a subject.
2. Herrick who never married penned some great love poems, addressing it to ladies, who may not have been real.

Answers

1. Influenced by Ben Jonson, Robert Herrick was a minister who took England's lush countryside as a subject.
2. Herrick, who never married, penned some great love poems, addressing them to ladies who may not have been real.

Day 4

Skills Practiced

- Correct use of preposition *like*
- Correct capitalization in title
- Correction of commonly confused words

Practice Sentences

1. As other Cavaliers, Richard Lovelace spent his personal fortune and many years in prison in support of King Charles.
2. "To Lucasta, on going to the Wars" exemplifies his principle theme, loyalty in love and war.

Answers

1. Like other Cavaliers, Richard Lovelace spent his personal fortune and many years in prison in support of King Charles.
2. "To Lucasta, on Going to the Wars" exemplifies his principal theme, loyalty in love and war.

Day 5

Skills Practiced

- Revision of wordy sentence
- Correction of run-on sentence
- Correction of commonly confused words
- Subject and verb agreement

Practice Sentences

1. In spite of the fact that he is remembered as a poet, Andrew Marvell's chief interest in life was his role in Parliament and representative government.
2. He wrote only a few poems, beneath there witty surface lies the serious concerns of a Puritan thinker.

Answers

1. Remembered as a poet, Andrew Marvell's chief interest in life was his role in Parliament and representative government.
2. He wrote only a few poems; beneath their witty surface lie the serious concerns of a Puritan thinker.

Daily Language Practice • Week 15

Day 1

Skills Practiced

Use of adverb to modify adverb

Use of active voice to improve style

Use of underlining or italics with words used as words

Capitalization of proper adjective

Practice Sentences

1. Curious enough, paradise has been viewed as a beautiful garden by poets and storytellers in different ages and cultures.

2. The word paradise itself comes from an old persian word meaning "a walled pleasure park."

Answers

1. Curiously enough, poets and storytellers in different ages and cultures have viewed paradise as a beautiful garden.

2. The word _paradise_ itself comes from an old Persian word meaning "a walled pleasure park."

Day 2

Skills Practiced

Use of underlining or italics with title of epic poem

Correct subordinating conjunction _as if_

Use of verb in the subjunctive mood

Use of hyphen in compound adjective

Practice Sentences

1. John Milton based his epic poem Paradise Lost on the biblical story of Adam and Eve and the Garden of Eden.

2. Milton describes Eden like it was a formal garden of a wealthy seventeenth century landowner.

Answers

1. John Milton based his epic poem _Paradise Lost_ on the biblical story of Adam and Eve and the Garden of Eden.

2. Milton describes Eden as if it were a formal garden of a wealthy seventeenth-century landowner.

Day 3

Skills Practiced

Use of commas with nonrestrictive clause

Eliminating _here_ after a demonstrative adjective

Correct formation of plural noun

Practice Sentences

1. In Greek myths the garden of the Hesperides where Atlas's daughters lived was paradise.

2. Central to this here garden was a tree with golden branchs and fruit, guarded fiercely by the inhabitants of the place.

Answers

1. In Greek myths the garden of the Hesperides, where Atlas's daughters lived, was paradise.

2. Central to this garden was a tree with golden branches and fruit, guarded fiercely by the inhabitants of the place.

Day 4

Skills Practiced

Pronoun agreement with antecedent

Subject and verb agreement

Use of commas with interrupter

Practice Sentences

1. Every culture has their own name for paradise, and neither evil nor sadness are ever found there.

2. When India becomes paradise according to some Buddhists it will effortlessly yield an abundance of fruits and flowers.

Answers

1. Every culture has its own name for paradise, and neither evil nor sadness is ever found there.

2. When India becomes paradise, according to some Buddhists, it will effortlessly yield an abundance of fruits and flowers.

Day 5

Skills Practiced

Subject and verb agreement

Correct use of colon before a list

Correct placement of comma with quotation marks

Capitalization of proper adjective

Practice Sentences

1. The long-lost garden paradise of some African tribes include the following, ample food, leisure time, and harmony with animals.

2. To find a well-hidden place called "the land without evil", the guarani tribe of South America conducts frequent trips to nearby territories.

Answers

1. The long-lost garden paradise of some African tribes includes the following: ample food, leisure time, and harmony with animals.

2. To find a well-hidden place called "the land without evil," the Guarani tribe of South America conducts frequent trips to nearby territories.

Daily Language Practice • Week 16

Day 1

Skills Practiced

Use of underlining or italics for a word used as a word

Use of quotation marks with direct quotation

Use of comma after introductory clause

Subject and verb agreement

Practice Sentences

1. The dictionary defines pilgrim as a person who journeys through foreign lands; a second meaning is one who travels to a holy place.

2. As you may remember <u>The Canterbury Tales</u> describe a group of travelers making a pilgrimage to a shrine.

Answers

1. The dictionary defines <u>pilgrim</u> as "a person who journeys through foreign lands"; a second meaning is "one who travels to a holy place."

2. As you may remember, <u>The Canterbury Tales</u> describes a group of travelers making a pilgrimage to a shrine.

Day 2

Skills Practiced

Subject and verb agreement

Use of commas to separate parts of an address

Use of commas with interrupter

Use of quotation marks to call attention to words or phrases

Practice Sentences

1. The proper noun <u>Pilgrims</u> refer to the English colonists who settled at Plymouth Massachusetts in 1620.

2. Until about 1820 however these colonists were known as Founders or Forefathers, not Pilgrims.

Answers

1. The proper noun <u>Pilgrims</u> refers to the English colonists who settled at Plymouth, Massachusetts, in 1620.

2. Until about 1820, however, these colonists were known as "Founders" or "Forefathers," not "Pilgrims."

	Skills Practiced	**Practice Sentences**

Day 3

Skills Practiced

Revision of choppy sentences

Correction of sentence fragment

Elimination of unnecessary words

Practice Sentences

1. The Pilgrim's Progress was a novel published in 1678. It was by John Bunyan. It popularized the concept of the pilgrim.
2. The main character, Christian, a pilgrim who encounters many adventures on his journey away from the City of Destruction off to the Celestial City.

Answers

1. The Pilgrim's Progress, a novel by John Bunyan published in 1678, popularized the concept of the pilgrim.
2. The main character, Christian, is a pilgrim who encounters many adventures on his journey from the City of Destruction to the Celestial City.

Day 4

Skills Practiced

Capitalization of proper noun

Elimination of *and* at the beginning of a sentence

Correct use of commas with nonrestrictive clause

Use of conjunctive adverb in compound sentence

Practice Sentences

1. Like the pilgrims who founded Plymouth, John Bunyan was a separatist in his religious views.
2. And to him, simplifying the Church of England from within as the Puritans hoped to do seemed futile; so he set up his own separate congregation.

Answers

1. Like the Pilgrims who founded Plymouth, John Bunyan was a Separatist in his religious views.
2. To him, simplifying the Church of England from within, as the Puritans hoped to do, seemed futile; therefore, he set up his own separate congregation.

Day 5

Skills Practiced

Revision of wordy sentence

Correction of commonly confused words

Capitalization of name of specific place

Spelling out numbers through one hundred

Use of active voice to improve style

Practice Sentences

1. Due to the fact that there's was an illegal religion, the Separatist Pilgrims fled first to Holland and later to the new world.
2. For his nonconformist views, John Bunyan spent 12 years in prison, where much of The Pilgrim's Progress was written.

Answers

1. Because theirs was an illegal religion, the Separatist Pilgrims fled first to Holland and later to the New World.
2. For his nonconformist views, John Bunyan spent twelve years in prison, where he wrote much of The Pilgrim's Progress.

Daily Language Practice • Week 17

Day 1

Skills Practiced

Correct use of conjunction

Use of parentheses to set off information

Use of commas in dates

Elimination of faulty parallel structure

Practice Sentences

1. Being as <u>The Diary of Samuel Pepys</u> pronounced PEEPS presents a personal look at seventeenth-century London, it is an invaluable resource.

2. Pepys wrote the diary from January 1 1660 to May 31 1669, using a combination of shorthand and encoding it.

Answers

1. Because <u>The Diary of Samuel Pepys</u> (pronounced PEEPS) presents a personal look at seventeenth-century London, it is an invaluable resource.

2. Pepys wrote the diary from January 1, 1660, to May 31, 1669, using a combination of shorthand and code.

Day 2

Skills Practiced

Use of colon to introduce clarifying information

Use of end punctuation: question mark

Use of adverb to modify a verb

Use of comma after introductory words

Practice Sentences

1. One question has always puzzled readers why did Pepys write his diary.

2. Almost certain his motive was to have a record of his young and busy life to reread and enjoy in his old age.

Answers

1. One question has always puzzled readers: Why did Pepys write his diary?

2. Almost certainly, his motive was to have a record of his young and busy life to reread and enjoy in his old age.

Day 3

Skills Practiced

Revision of stringy sentence

Capitalization of name of organization

Correction of commonly misused words

Correct past form of irregular verb

Practice Sentences

1. Pepys was a naval official, and he had a cousin who was an earl, and he was the president of the royal society.

2. To the great and small events of his day, Pepys took his keen eye and genial personality and done a good job of recording information.

Answers

1. A naval official and a cousin to an earl, Pepys was the president of the Royal Society.

2. To the great and small events of his day, Pepys brought his keen eye and genial personality and did a good job of recording information.

Day 4

Skills Practiced

Formation of singular possessive

Use of commas in a date

Use of adverb to modify a verb

Correct pronoun case

Practice Sentences

1. Samuel Pepys entry for September 2 1666 describes a great fire that damaged London bad.

2. His family, friends, and him also lived through a plague that killed thousands.

Answers

1. Samuel Pepys's entry for September 2, 1666, describes a great fire that damaged London badly.

2. His family, friends, and he also lived through a plague that killed thousands.

Day 5

Skills Practiced

Correction of commonly confused words

Correct use of helping verb *have*

Use of verb in the subjunctive mood

Subject and verb agreement

Use of adverb to modify verb

Practice Sentences

1. Loosing his sight in middle age, Samuel Pepys couldn't of reread his diary in his later years.

2. However, if Pepys was to know that a large audience enjoy his diary today, he would sure be happy.

Answers

1. Losing his sight in middle age, Samuel Pepys couldn't have reread his diary in his later years.

2. However, if Pepys were to know that a large audience enjoys his diary today, he would surely be happy.

Daily Language Practice • Week 18

Day 1

Skills Practiced

Use of present perfect tense

Use of underlining or italics with foreign words

Elimination of unnecessary word

Use of *between* and *among*

Correct use of reflexive pronoun

Practice Sentences

1. Throughout history, terrible epidemics of bubonic plague swept through Europe, Asia, and Africa.

2. The germ Pasteurella pestis causes the disease; fleas from infected rats transmit it over to humans, who spread it between theirselves by coughing.

Answers

1. Throughout history, terrible epidemics of bubonic plague have swept through Europe, Asia, and Africa.

2. The germ <u>Pasteurella pestis</u> causes the disease; fleas from infected rats transmit it to humans, who spread it among themselves by coughing.

Day 2

Skills Practiced

Spelling out numbers through one hundred

Subject and verb agreement

Correction of misplaced modifier

Use of strong noun to improve style

Practice Sentences

1. The plague germ, which was discovered in 1894, works fast; sometimes only 3 or 4 days passes between the onset of the disease and the victim's death.

2. During the 1300's historians estimate that three quarters of Europe's population were lost to the plague.

Answers

1. The plague germ, which was discovered in 1894, works fast; sometimes only three or four days pass between the onset of the disease and the victim's death.

2. Historians estimate that three quarters of Europe's population were plague victims during the 1300's.

Day 3

Skills Practiced

Use of commas in large numerals

Elimination of split infinitive

Use of past perfect tense

Correct spelling of plural noun

Practice Sentences

1. In the 1600's, when some 150000 Londoners died of plague, quarantine measures helped to somewhat contain the disease.

2. If doctors understood the disease better, they would have saved more lifes.

Answers

1. In the 1600's, when some 150,000 Londoners died of plague, quarantine measures helped to contain the disease somewhat.

2. If doctors had understood the disease better, they would have saved more lives.

Day 4

Skills Practiced

Use of apostrophe to form possessive

Correct use of intensive pronoun

Use of semicolon to correct run-on sentence

Correct use of indefinite article

Practice Sentences

1. A Journal of the Plague Year is Daniel Defoes account of London's 1665 plague.

2. Novelist Defoe did not experience the plague hisself, his 1771 work is a early example of fiction appearing as a report from firsthand observation.

Answers

1. A Journal of the Plague Year is Daniel Defoe's account of London's 1665 plague.

2. Novelist Defoe did not experience the plague himself; his 1771 work is an early example of fiction appearing as a report from firsthand observation.

Day 5

Skills Practiced

Use of numerals and words for round numbers ending in millions

Elimination of empty sentence

Use of comma after introductory words

Elimination of faulty parallel structure

Practice Sentences

1. The most disastrous modern outbreak of plague killed 10,000,000 people in India early this century. This was devastating.

2. Since then measures such as antibiotics, strict quarantines, and exterminating rats have controlled but not eliminated the bubonic plague.

Answers

1. The most disastrous modern outbreak of plague killed 10 million people in India early this century.

2. Since then, measures such as antibiotics, strict quarantines, and rat extermination have controlled but not eliminated the bubonic plague.

Daily Language Practice • Week 19

Day 1

Skills Practiced

Use of *that* in restrictive clause

Use of precise adjective to improve style

Use of comma with nonrestrictive clause

Correct formation of possessive

Correct use of coordinating conjunction

Practice Sentences

1. Deeply concerned about humanity, Jonathan Swift ridiculed ideas and habits which he considered bad.

2. In Gulliver's Travels, Swift created a masterpiece which can be read as a childrens' fantasy but a sophisticated satire of English life and politics too.

Answers

1. Deeply concerned about humanity, Jonathan Swift ridiculed ideas and habits that he considered harmful.

2. In Gulliver's Travels, Swift created a masterpiece, which can be read as a children's fantasy or a sophisticated satire of English life and politics.

Day 2

Skills Practiced

Subject and verb agreement

Use of quotation marks to call attention to specific words or phrases

Use of commas with nonrestrictive clause

Practice Sentences

1. Gulliver's Travels describe four voyages that Lemuel Gulliver, a ship's doctor, makes to some far-out places.

2. Landing in Lilliput where everyone is one-twelfth his size he finds absurd political and religious controversies that mimic those of England.

Answers

1. Gulliver's Travels describes four voyages that Lemuel Gulliver, a ship's doctor, makes to some "far-out" places.

2. Landing in Lilliput, where everyone is one-twelfth his size, he finds absurd political and religious controversies that mimic those of England.

Day 3

Skills Practiced

Spelling out numbers through one hundred

Use of predicate adjective after linking verb

Correct spelling of homophones

Use of hyphen with prefix *self-*

Practice Sentences

1. Gulliver travels next to Brobdingnag, where people are 12 times his size; these giants feel badly when they here about life in England.

2. In size and nature, the Brobdingnagians contrast sharply with the small-mindedness of petty and selfserving Europeans.

Answers

1. Gulliver travels next to Brobdingnag, where people are twelve times his size; these giants feel bad when they hear about life in England.

2. In size and nature, the Brobdingnagians contrast sharply with the small-mindedness of petty and self-serving Europeans.

Day 4

Skills Practiced

Correction of commonly misused words

Correct use of possessive pronoun

Use of comma after introductory infinitive phrase

Practice Sentences

1. Gulliver voyages further to lands who's inhabitants display types of foolishness that Swift condemned.

2. To satirize the impracticality of some scientists he describes an academy where scholars spend all their time getting sunbeams from cucumbers.

Answers

1. Gulliver voyages farther to lands whose inhabitants display types of foolishness that Swift condemned.

2. To satirize the impracticality of some scientists, he describes an academy where scholars spend all their time getting sunbeams from cucumbers.

Day 5

Skills Practiced

Elimination of redundancy

Use of commas with coordinate adjectives

Elimination of *here* after a demonstrative adjective

Use of end punctuation: question mark

Practice Sentences

1. On his last final voyage, Gulliver discovers the wise perfect horses called Houyhnhnms and the savage humanlike Yahoos.

2. Was the wild contrast between these here two groups Swift's way of advising us to avoid extremes and live moderate lives.

Answers

1. On his final voyage, Gulliver discovers the wise, perfect horses called Houyhnhnms and the savage, humanlike Yahoos.

2. Was the wild contrast between these two groups Swift's way of advising us to avoid extremes and live moderate lives?

Day 1

Skills Practiced

Capitalization of title before person's name

Pronoun agreement with antecedent

Correct spelling: addition of suffix -*ness*

Practice Sentences

1. When sir Isaac Newton's laws of motion and theory of gravitation were published in 1687, it had a profound effect on intellectual life.

2. With thrilling suddeness, Newton's work seemed to reveal the underlying order and harmony of nature's laws.

Answers

1. When Sir Isaac Newton's laws of motion and theory of gravitation were published in 1687, they had a profound effect on intellectual life.

2. With thrilling suddenness, Newton's work seemed to reveal the underlying order and harmony of nature's laws.

Day 2

Skills Practiced

Use of commas to set off appositive

Elimination of double subject

Use of colon to introduce a clarifying idea

Pronoun agreement with antecedent

Practice Sentences

1. A new age the Enlightenment was dawning in Europe, and science and reason they were its major themes.

2. New discoveries in astronomy, physics, and chemistry led to one conclusion humankind would soon perfect their knowledge of the world.

Answers

1. A new age, the Enlightenment, was dawning in Europe, and science and reason were its major themes.

2. New discoveries in astronomy, physics, and chemistry led to one conclusion: humankind would soon perfect its knowledge of the world.

Day 3

Skills Practiced

Subject and verb agreement

Capitalization of historical period

Revision of sentence ending with a preposition

Practice Sentences

1. Economics were another field that enlightenment thinkers thought should be as rational as pure science.

2. Evidence of the laws that controlled all human activity is what they looked for.

Answers

1. Economics was another field that Enlightenment thinkers thought should be as rational as pure science.

2. They looked for evidence of the laws that controlled all human activity.

Day 4

Skills Practiced

Use of participial phrase to combine sentences

Correct formation of irregular verb tense

Use of comma after introductory participial phrase

Capitalization of name of historic event

Practice Sentences

1. Inventors and investors were encouraged by a growing confidence in human abilities. They designed and builded new technologies.

2. Put to work in this way the ideas of the Enlightenment gave rise to the industrial revolution in England.

Answers

1. Encouraged by a growing confidence in human abilities, inventors and investors designed and built new technologies.

2. Put to work in this way, the ideas of the Enlightenment gave rise to the Industrial Revolution in England.

Day 5

Skills Practiced

Use of hyphen in word broken at end of a line

Use of proper adjectives

Elimination of *you* without a clear antecedent

Elimination of split infinitive

Practice Sentences

1. In their search for harmony, Enlightenment poets emulated classi cal Greece and Rome writings.

2. You also sense that they satirized the forces that seemed to often stand in the way of reason and progress.

Answers

1. In their search for harmony, Enlightenment poets emulated classi-cal Greek and Roman writings.

2. Readers also sense that they satirized the forces that seemed often to stand in the way of reason and progress.

Daily Language Practice • Week 21

Day 1

Skills Practiced

Correct use of semicolon and comma with a conjunctive adverb to correct run-on sentence

Spelling out ordinal numbers

Capitalization of name of historical period

Use of verb in the subjunctive mood

Practice Sentences

1. Samuel Johnson was a very influential literary figure, in fact the second half of the 18th century in England is often called the age of Johnson.

2. Was it not for James Boswell, the author's biographer and friend, much of Johnson's wit and brilliance might have been lost.

Answers

1. Samuel Johnson was a very influential literary figure; in fact, the second half of the eighteenth century in England is often called the Age of Johnson.

2. Were it not for James Boswell, the author's biographer and friend, much of Johnson's wit and brilliance might have been lost.

Day 2

Skills Practiced

Correction of an illogical comparison

Use of dashes to set off additional information

Use of semicolon to correct run-on sentence

Use of commas in a series

Practice Sentences

1. Better known than any lexicographer, Johnson is remembered for his massive—and in some definitions, humorous <u>Dictionary of the English Language</u>.

2. Johnson compiled his dictionary between 1746 and 1755, during those years he also wrote essays poems and criticism.

Answers

1. Better known than any other lexicographer, Johnson is remembered for his massive—and in some definitions, humorous—<u>Dictionary of the English Language.</u>

2. Johnson compiled his dictionary between 1746 and 1755; during those years he also wrote essays, poems, and criticism.

Day 3

Skills Practiced

Correct pronoun case

Revision of awkward phrasing

Use of past perfect tense

Correction of commonly confused words

Practice Sentences

1. James Boswell, to who Johnson was a mentor, diligently filled notebooks with his friend's conversation.

2. Then, long after the events occurred, Boswell adopted his notes into a unified work of art and a new type of biography.

Answers

1. James Boswell, to whom Johnson was a mentor, diligently filled notebooks with his friend's conversation.

2. Then, long after the events had occurred, Boswell adapted his notes into a unified work of art and a new type of biography.

Day 4

Skills Practiced

Use of italics or underlining for title of book

Pronoun agreement with antecedent

Correction of unclear pronoun reference

Use of subordinating conjunction to combine sentences

Practice Sentences

1. Unlike earlier biographies, The Life of Samuel Johnson by James Boswell did not glorify his subject by hiding his faults.

2. Even the greatest people have shortcomings. Boswell hoped that readers would avoid his follies while copying his virtues.

Answers

1. Unlike earlier biographies, <u>The Life of Samuel Johnson</u> by James Boswell did not glorify its subject by hiding Dr. Johnson's faults.

2. Since even the greatest people have shortcomings, Boswell hoped that readers would avoid Johnson's follies while copying his virtues.

Day 5

Skills Practiced

Revision of subordinating conjunction

Correction of commonly confused words

Use of specific noun to improve style

Elimination of superlative form with absolute adjective

Correct superlative form of an adjective

Practice Sentences

1. Boswell's biography of Johnson was also a historical first inasmuch as that it presented a bunch of particular details rather then a generalized overview.

2. Boswell's most supreme achievement is the preservation of the words of one of England's most great thinkers and speakers.

Answers

1. Boswell's biography of Johnson was also a historic first since it presented a wealth of particular details rather than a generalized overview.

2. Boswell's supreme achievement is the preservation of the words of one of England's greatest thinkers and speakers.

Daily Language Practice • Week 22

Day 1

Skills Practiced

Use of comma after introductory participial phrase

Inclusion of closing quotation marks

Use of hyphen with the prefix *self-*

Possessive form of name ending in *s*

Capitalization of name of holiday

Use of quotation marks with title of song

Practice Sentences

1. Often called "the voice of Scotland Robert Burns was largely self educated and spent most of his life as a farmer.

2. Burns many well-known poems and songs include the new year's eve favorite Auld Lang Syne.

Answers

1. Often called "the voice of Scotland," Robert Burns was largely self-educated and spent most of his life as a farmer.

2. Burns's many well-known poems and songs include the New Year's Eve favorite "Auld Lang Syne."

Day 2

Skills Practiced

Correct spelling: doubling final consonant

Use of dash to set off additional information

Use of hyphen in compound adjective

Use of correlative conjunction

Practice Sentences

1. Rebeling against formal eighteenth-century poetry, Burns wrote about everyday subjects, farm work, family life, and even mice and lice!

2. His use of the Scottish dialect not only brought a much needed freshness to English poetry and honored common men and women.

Answers

1. Rebelling against formal eighteenth-century poetry, Burns wrote about everyday subjects—farm work, family life, and even mice and lice!

2. His use of the Scottish dialect not only brought a much-needed freshness to English poetry but also honored common men and women.

Day 3

Skills Practiced

- Capitalization of first word in a line of poetry
- Use of underlining or italics with foreign words
- Use of commas with interrupter

Practice Sentences

1. Many of Burns's lines, such as "the best laid schemes o' mice and men/ gang aft agley," have become familiar quotations.
2. "Gang aft agley" by the way is Scottish dialect for "often go wrong."

Answers

1. Many of Burns's lines, such as "The best laid schemes o' mice and men/ Gang aft agley," have become familiar quotations.
2. _Gang aft agley_, by the way, is Scottish dialect for "often go wrong."

Day 4

Skills Practiced

- Correction of dangling modifier
- Use of active voice to improve style
- Elimination of unnecessary preposition
- Use of semicolon to correct run-on sentences

Practice Sentences

1. Keenly interested in Scottish folk music, poems by Robert Burns were intended to be sung to traditional tunes.
2. Not all of the poet's work was in dialect, when dealing with more typical or respectable subject matter, Burns wrote in standard English.

Answers

1. Keenly interested in Scottish folk music, Burns intended people to sing his poems to traditional tunes.
2. Not all the poet's work was in dialect; when dealing with more typical or respectable subject matter, Burns wrote in standard English.

Day 5

Skills Practiced

- Elimination of unnecessary comma in compound construction
- Use of adverb to modify a verb
- Use of comma to set off absolute phrase
- Correction of commonly misspelled word

Practice Sentences

1. Robert Burns enjoyed a few seasons of fame, but suffered bad from poverty and illness all his life.
2. No matter what the feelings in his heart Burns captured them in the versetile and vigorous language of his poetry.

Answers

1. Robert Burns enjoyed a few seasons of fame but suffered badly from poverty and illness all his life.
2. No matter what the feelings in his heart, Burns captured them in the versatile and vigorous language of his poetry.

Daily Language Practice • Week 23

Day 1

Skills Practiced

Use of coordinating conjunction to correct run-on sentence

Correct past participle of irregular verb

Elimination of question mark with indirect question

Practice Sentences

1. By the late 1700's, the Enlightenment, with its emphasis on reason and classical studies, had run its course, a new artistic movement had arose.

2. Proponents of Romanticism asked why people shouldn't experience the world through the heart instead of the mind?

Answers

1. By the late 1700's, the Enlightenment, with its emphasis on reason and classical studies, had run its course, and a new artistic movement had arisen.

2. Proponents of Romanticism asked why people shouldn't experience the world through the heart instead of the mind.

Day 2

Skills Practiced

Use of past perfect tense

Use of comma after day and year in a date

Combining sentences

Use of commas to set off adjectives following noun

Use of comma to set off appositive

Practice Sentences

1. Romantics cheered the French Revolution, which began on July 14 1789. It changed Europe's political landscape forever.

2. That revolution bloody and destructive would improve the lives of common people; a concern of the Romantics.

Answers

1. Romantics cheered the French Revolution, which had begun on July 14, 1789, and changed Europe's political landscape forever.

2. That revolution, bloody and destructive, would improve the lives of common people, a concern of the Romantics.

Day 3

Skills Practiced

Use of *different from*

Subject and verb agreement

Use of semicolons in a series containing commas

Practice Sentences

1. Entirely different than the poetic style it replaced, Romanticism's spontaneity and excess was legendary.

2. The Romantics were interested in local history, folktales, and legends, the mysterious, the imaginative, and the supernatural, and any new form of expression.

Answers

1. Entirely different from the poetic style it replaced, Romanticism's tendency toward spontaneity and excess was legendary.

2. The Romantics were interested in local history, folktales, and legends; the mysterious, the imaginative, and the supernatural; and any new form of expression.

Day 4

Skills Practiced

Use of semicolon to correct run-on sentence

Correction of misplaced participial phrase

Use of quotation marks in a split quotation

Practice Sentences

1. Romanticism stresses individual freedom the romantic hero often becomes a rebel or outlaw, rejecting restrictive social conventions.

2. "Man is born free, the Romantic philosopher Jean-Jacques Rousseau wrote, and everywhere he is in chains."

Answers

1. Romanticism stresses individual freedom; the romantic hero, rejecting restrictive social conventions, often becomes a rebel or outlaw.

2. "Man is born free," the Romantic philosopher Jean-Jacques Rousseau wrote, "and everywhere he is in chains."

Day 5

Skills Practiced

Use of prepositional phrase to combine sentences

Revision of wordy sentence

Correction of *they* without a clear antecedent

Practice Sentences

1. Romantic painters used bold lighting effects and deep shadows to portray their exotic subjects. They portrayed them in faraway settings too.

2. In many pieces of romantic music they often used folksongs as themes and stressed lyricism over formalism.

Answers

1. Romantic painters used bold lighting effects and deep shadows to portray their exotic subjects in faraway settings.

2. Composers of romantic music often used folksongs as themes and stressed lyricism over formalism.

Daily Language Practice • Week 24

Day 1

Skills Practiced

Elimination of redundancy

Use of past perfect tense

Use of a comma after introductory phrases

Correct pronoun case

Practice Sentences

1. For William Wordsworth, poetry was an imaginative way for him to express emotions that came from his personal experiences.

2. In an 1802 preface to <u>Lyrical Ballads</u> Samuel Taylor Coleridge and him outlined ideas that are now identified with Romanticism.

Answers

1. For William Wordsworth, poetry was an imaginative way to express emotions that had come from his personal experiences.

2. In an 1802 preface to <u>Lyrical Ballads</u>, Samuel Taylor Coleridge and he outlined ideas that are now identified with Romanticism.

Day 2

Skills Practiced

Use of commas with interrupter

Use of semicolon and comma with conjunctive adverb to correct run-on sentence

Correction of commonly confused words

Elimination of unnecessary prepositions

Practice Sentences

1. Wordsworth's personality to say nothing of his poetry was shaped by nature.

2. The human mind was his primary interest however, his poems illustrate how the imagination may create spiritual values from out of nature's sights and sounds.

Answers

1. Wordsworth's personality, to say nothing of his poetry, was shaped by nature.

2. The human mind was his primary interest; however, his poems illustrate how the imagination can create spiritual values from nature's sights and sounds.

Day 3

Skills Practiced

Capitalization of name of specific building

Use of possessive case with gerund

Use of *different from*

Correction of sentence fragment

Practice Sentences

1. When Wordsworth revisited Tintern abbey after five years, it looking so different than what he remembered puzzled him.

2. Struck by the discrepancy between memory and perception. Wordsworth meditated on his past, present, and future.

Answers

1. When Wordsworth revisited Tintern Abbey after five years, its looking so different from what he remembered puzzled him.

2. Struck by the discrepancy between memory and perception, Wordsworth meditated on his past, present, and future.

Day 4

Skills Practiced

Use of comma before coordinating conjunction in compound sentence

Correct pronoun case

Use of comma to set off appositive

Use of correct form of reflexive pronoun

Practice Sentences

1. At Tintern Abbey, Wordsworth sensed that this world would never really be intelligible for both him and his perceptions were constantly changing.

2. Nevertheless, using nature as a guide, Wordsworth sought to see into "the life of things"; an unchanging, underlying world of things in theirselves.

Answers

1. At Tintern Abbey, Wordsworth sensed that this world would never really be intelligible, for both he and his perceptions were constantly changing.

2. Nevertheless, using nature as a guide, Wordsworth sought to see into "the life of things," an unchanging, underlying world of things in themselves.

Day 5

Skills Practiced

Verb tense compatibility

Correction of commonly confused words

Revision of choppy sentences

Practice Sentences

1. William Wordsworth elaborated no consistent philosophical system in his poetry; his thoughts come from brilliant flashes of intuition.

2. Wordsworth's greatness lied in his ability to group details into a poetic pattern. These are details that everyone recognizes. This is a pattern that brings out inner truth.

Answers

1. William Wordsworth elaborated no consistent philosophical system in his poetry; his thoughts came from brilliant flashes of intuition.

2. Wordsworth's greatness lay in his ability to group details that everyone recognizes into a poetic pattern that brings out inner truth.

Daily Language Practice • Week 25

Day 1

Skills Practiced

- Elimination of commas with a restrictive appositive
- Correction of commonly confused words
- Elimination of unnecessary hyphens in compound modifier
- Correction of unclear pronoun reference

Practice Sentences

1. In his masterpiece, <u>The Rime of the Ancient Mariner</u>, Samuel Taylor Coleridge tells a vivid story with startling affects.

2. The running commentary in the margins, added later by the poet, is easy-to-read and serves as a guide to its philosophy.

Answers

1. In his masterpiece <u>The Rime of the Ancient Mariner</u>, Samuel Taylor Coleridge tells a vivid story with startling effects.

2. The running commentary in the margins, added later by the poet, is easy to read and serves as a guide to the poet's philosophy.

Day 2

Skills Practiced

- Correct relative pronoun and punctuation in nonrestrictive clause
- Elimination of *you* without a clear antecedent
- Use of specific noun to improve style
- Use of quotation marks in a split quotation

Practice Sentences

1. <u>The Rime of the Ancient Mariner</u> combines the vivid imagery and intricate symbolism, which you might expect in something based on a dream.

2. "I readily believe, read a Latin quotation that opened an early edition of the poem that there are more invisible than visible Natures in the universe."

Answers

1. <u>The Rime of the Ancient Mariner</u> combines the vivid imagery and intricate symbolism that a reader might expect in a poem based on a dream.

2. "I readily believe," read a Latin quotation that opened an early edition of the poem, "that there are more invisible than visible Natures in the universe."

Day 3

Skills Practiced

Subject and verb agreement

Revision of wordy sentence

Elimination of unnecessary hyphen in compound modifier

Practice Sentences

1. The blending of ordinary and supernatural elements in The Rime of the Ancient Mariner show Coleridge's interest in romantic subjects.

2. In light of the consideration of the fact that Coleridge's other famous poems were unfinished, the skillfully-constructed and unified Rime is all the more striking.

Answers

1. The blending of ordinary and supernatural elements in The Rime of the Ancient Mariner shows Coleridge's interest in romantic subjects.

2. Since Coleridge's other famous poems were unfinished, the skillfully constructed and unified Rime is all the more striking.

Day 4

Skills Practiced

Revision of choppy sentences

Correction of sentence fragment

Correction of misplaced modifier

Practice Sentences

1. Coleridge uses the stanza format of a ballad. He unfolds the mariner's complex story. He does so in a direct fashion.

2. To produce emotional and musical effects, such as alliteration, consonance, and assonance, are among the poetic devices used.

Answers

1. Using the stanza format of a ballad, Coleridge unfolds the mariner's complex story in a direct fashion.

2. Among the poetic devices used to produce emotional and musical effects are alliteration, consonance, and assonance.

Day 5

Skills Practiced

Use of numerals for numbers above one hundred

Use of colon to introduce clarifying material

Use of hyphen with prefix *all-*

Correct format of a longer quotation

Capitalization of first word in line of poetry

Practice Sentences

1. Coleridge's six-hundred-and-twenty-five-line narrative poem ends on an optimistic note, love is all important.

2. Near the end, Coleridge pronounces his faith, "He prayeth best who loveth best / all things both great and small...."

Answers

1. Coleridge's 625-line narrative poem ends on an optimistic note: love is all-important.

2. Near the end, Coleridge pronounces his faith:
    "He prayeth best who loveth best
    All things both great and small...."

Daily Language Practice • Week 26

Day 1

Skills Practiced

Elimination of split infinitive

Subject and verb agreement

Correction of misplaced modifier

Capitalization of important words in a title

Practice Sentences

1. For John Keats, using the senses to fully appreciate beauty lead to an understanding of ultimate truth.

2. The line "Beauty is truth, truth beauty" sums up this understanding at the end of "Ode On a Grecian urn."

Answers

1. For John Keats, using the senses to appreciate beauty fully leads to an understanding of ultimate truth.

2. The line "Beauty is truth, truth beauty" at the end of "Ode on a Grecian Urn" sums up this understanding.

Day 2

Skills Practiced

Pronoun agreement with antecedent

Use of adverb to modify a verb

Revision of wordy sentence

Practice Sentences

1. John Keats took intense delight in objects around him, contemplating it so close that he would seem to lose his own identity.

2. Although Keats is considered a poet of sensuous beauty, it was the truth behind his sensations that mattered most to him.

Answers

1. John Keats took intense delight in objects around him, contemplating them so closely that he would seem to lose his own identity.

2. Although Keats is considered a poet of sensuous beauty, the truth behind his sensations mattered most to him.

Day 3

Skills Practiced

Possessive form of name ending in s

Elimination of redundancy

Correction of commonly misspelled word

Combining sentences

Practice Sentences

1. "On First Looking into Chapman's Homer" expresses Keats' strong feeling of ecstacy upon reading Homer's poetry.

2. "Ode on a Grecian Urn" reveals a Keats haunted by the inevitable passing of beauty. So does "To Autumn."

Answers

1. "On First Looking into Chapman's Homer" expresses Keats's ecstasy upon reading Homer's poetry.

2. "Ode on a Grecian Urn" and "To Autumn" reveal a Keats haunted by the inevitable passing of beauty.

Day 4

Skills Practiced

Elimination of commonly misused word

Subject and verb agreement

Use of end punctuation: question mark

Practice Sentences

1. In "Ode to a Nightingale," a bird's sweet song literally calls the speaker away from the cares of human life and into the essence of natural beauty.

2. Is the speaker's senses a bridge between the sad world he inhabits and the eternal world he imagines.

Answers

1. In "Ode to a Nightingale," a bird's sweet song calls the speaker away from the cares of human life and into the essence of natural beauty.

2. Are the speaker's senses a bridge between the sad world he inhabits and the eternal world he imagines?

Day 5

Skills Practiced

Elimination of faulty parallel structure

Correction of run-on sentence

Use of colon to introduce material that clarifies a preceding statement

Practice Sentences

1. In spite of poverty, illness, and being rejected by critics, Keats remained devoted to his poetry and constantly searching for truth in personal experience.

2. Tragically, Keats died at age twenty-five no name appears on his tombstone, only this epitaph, "Here lies one whose name was writ in water."

Answers

1. In spite of poverty, illness, and rejection by critics, Keats remained devoted to his poetry and the constant search for truth in personal experience.

2. Tragically, Keats died at age twenty-five. No name appears on his tombstone, only this epitaph: "Here lies one whose name was writ in water."

Daily Language Practice • Week 27

Day 1

Skills Practiced

Use of commas with nonrestrictive clause

Correction of commonly confused words

Use of specific term to improve style

Capitalization of name of proper adjective

Elimination of unnecessary exclamation point

Practice Sentences

1. The Industrial Revolution, which began in England during the 1700's and spread to Europe and North America was a historical happening.

2. By the mid-1800's, western society, once rural and agricultural, had become urban and industrial!

Answers

1. The Industrial Revolution, which began in England during the 1700's and spread to Europe and North America, was a historic turning point.

2. By the mid-1800's, Western society, once rural and agricultural, had become urban and industrial.

Day 2

Skills Practiced

Capitalization of name of historical period

Verb tense compatibility

Use of semicolons in a series containing commas

Practice Sentences

1. New inventions made the industrial revolution possible, while improvements in transportation and finance allow it to continue.

2. The new inventions included the steam engine, textile machinery, such as the spinning jenny and flying shuttle, and puddling furnaces, coke smelters, and other iron-making techniques.

Answers

1. New inventions made the Industrial Revolution possible, while improvements in transportation and finance allowed it to continue.

2. The new inventions included the steam engine; textile machinery, such as the spinning jenny and flying shuttle; and puddling furnaces, coke smelters, and other iron-making techniques.

Day 3

Skills Practiced

Use of precise adjectives to improve style

Correction of faulty subordination

Use of commas to set off antithetical element

Subject and verb agreement

Practice Sentences

1. With its good factories, Britain became a great manufacturer; factory towns grew into large cities when banks and other businesses expanded.
2. The British navy to say nothing of fleets of merchant ships were also expanding, allowing the British to acquire new colonies in Africa and Asia.

Answers

1. With its advanced factories, Britain became a leading manufacturer; when factory towns grew into large cities, banks and other businesses expanded.
2. The British navy, to say nothing of fleets of merchant ships, was also expanding, allowing the British to acquire new colonies in Africa and Asia.

Day 4

Skills Practiced

Use of comma to separate identical words

Correction of commonly misspelled word

Use of commas after introductory phrases

Practice Sentences

1. By the end of the Industrial Revolution, whatever educational and political privileges the aristocracy had had been extended to the growing middle class.
2. Before the 1800's the upper classes controlled Parlament; after the 1800's the middle classes did.

Answers

1. By the end of the Industrial Revolution, whatever educational and political privileges the aristocracy had, had been extended to the growing middle class.
2. Before the 1800's, the upper classes controlled Parliament; after the 1800's, the middle classes did.

Day 5

Skills Practiced

Use of quotation marks with slang

Use of colon before a list

Streamlining sentences with possessive forms

Practice Sentences

1. The Industrial Revolution created some monsters; sweatshops, slums, child labor, pollution.
2. The new realities of society would become the concerns of Parliament and the subject matter of many authors.

Answers

1. The Industrial Revolution created some "monsters": sweatshops, slums, child labor, pollution.
2. Society's new realities would become Parliament's concerns and many authors' subject matter.

Daily Language Practice • Week 28

Day 1

Skills Practiced

Verb tense compatibility

Formation of irregular plural noun

Possessive form of name ending in *s*

Use of hyphen in compound adjective

Practice Sentences

1. Charles Dickens sympathizes with the downtrodden in society and waged a literary campaign against selfishness and cruelty.

2. Early crisises in the author's life may have prompted his desire to improve society; Dicken's father's debts landed him in jail, and twelve year old Charles had to go to work in a factory.

Answers

1. Charles Dickens sympathized with the downtrodden in society and waged a literary campaign against selfishness and cruelty.

2. Early crises in the author's life may have prompted his desire to improve society; Dickens's father's debts landed him in jail, and twelve-year-old Charles had to go to work in a factory.

Day 2

Skills Practiced

Elimination of unnecessary exclamation point

Subject and verb agreement

Elimination of unnecessary preposition

Correct spelling: addition of suffix *-ness*

Practice Sentences

1. The title character of <u>Oliver Twist</u>, Dickens's second novel, is a young, mistreated orphan involved in London's criminal underworld!

2. There are, as always in Dickens, enough of humor to keep the story entertaining despite the solemness of the problems it depicts.

Answers

1. The title character of <u>Oliver Twist</u>, Dickens's second novel, is a young, mistreated orphan involved in London's criminal underworld.

2. There is, always in Dickens, enough humor to keep the story entertaining despite the solemnness of the problems it depicts.

Day 3

Skills Practiced

Elimination of an illogical comparison

Elimination of superlative with absolute adjective

Use of vivid verb to improve style

Elimination of redundancy

Practice Sentences

1. Most critics claim <u>Bleak House</u> is better than any novel by Dickens because of its most unique structure and many levels of meaning.

2. An attack on wasteful legal processes, <u>Bleak House</u> also talks about a range of social ills ranging from false humanitarians to poor sanitation.

Answers

1. Most critics claim <u>Bleak House</u> is better than any other novel by Dickens because of its unique structure and many levels of meaning.

2. An attack on wasteful legal processes, <u>Bleak House</u> also exposes other social ills ranging from false humanitarians to poor sanitation.

Day 4

Skills Practiced

Correction of commonly misused words

Use of end punctuation: question mark

Use of correct form of reflexive pronoun

Practice Sentences

1. Who has not heard of the miser Ebenezer Scrooge in <u>A Christmas Carol</u>, who's greed has cut him off from human love.

2. In <u>Dombey and Son</u>, Dickens again turns to this theme, showing how family members become embittered among theirselves over money.

Answers

1. Who has not heard of the miser Ebenezer Scrooge in <u>A Christmas Carol</u>, whose greed has cut him off from human love?

2. In <u>Dombey and Son</u>, Dickens again turns to this theme, showing how family members become embittered among themselves over money.

Day 5

Skills Practiced

Subject and verb agreement

Use of subordination to correct run-on sentence

Correction of commonly misspelled word

Use of apostrophes to indicate separate possession

Practice Sentences

1. <u>Great Expectations</u> explore the values of its young hero, Pip, he gradually learns to base his life on true human sympathy.

2. The author's last novel, <u>Our Mutual Friend</u>, again criticizes goverment and people's hypocrisies.

Answers

1. <u>Great Expectations</u> explores the values of its young hero, Pip, who gradually learns to base his life on true human sympathy.

2. The author's last novel, <u>Our Mutual Friend</u>, again criticizes government's and people's hypocrisies.

Daily Language Practice • Week 29

<table>
<tr><td>Day 1</td><td>

Skills Practiced

Subject and verb agreement

Use of commas to set off appositives

Elimination of *you* without a clear antecedent

</td><td>

Practice Sentences

1. The number and types of beats in a line determines a poem's meter its rhythmic pattern.

2. Counting and marking the stressed and unstressed syllables in each line a process called scanning allows you to identify a poem's meter.

Answers

1. The number and types of beats in a line determine a poem's meter, its rhythmic pattern.

2. Counting and marking the stressed and unstressed syllables in each line, a process called scanning, allows a reader to identify a poem's meter.

</td></tr>
<tr><td>Day 2</td><td>

Skills Practiced

Correction of faulty subordination

Elimination of commas with restrictive clause

Use of comma to indicate parallel phrase

</td><td>

Practice Sentences

1. Modern poetry that is called free verse does not have a regular meter.

2. Scanning a poem, that is written in meter, involves marking each stressed syllable with an accent ('); each unstressed syllable with a breve (˘).

Answers

1. Modern poetry that does not have a regular meter is called free verse.

2. Scanning a poem that is written in meter involves marking each stressed syllable with an accent ('), each unstressed syllable with a breve (˘).

</td></tr>
</table>

Day 3

Skills Practiced

Streamlining sentence with use of possessive

Correct use of colon before a list

Use of commas with nonrestrictive appositives

Practice Sentences

1. The meter of a poem is identified with a vertical line dividing the stressed and unstressed syllables into groups called poetic feet.

2. Two common types of poetic feet are: the iamb a stressed syllable followed by an unstressed one, and the trochee an unstressed syllable followed by a stressed one.

Answers

1. A poem's meter is identified with a vertical line dividing the stressed and unstressed syllables into groups called poetic feet.

2. Here are two common types of poetic feet: the iamb, a stressed syllable followed by an unstressed one, and the trochee, an unstressed syllable followed by a stressed one.

Day 4

Skills Practiced

Subject and verb agreement

Use of hyphens with compound modifiers

Use of quotation marks with title of an essay

Practice Sentences

1. The number of feet in a line determine the meter; trimeter is written in three foot lines, tetrameter in four foot lines, and so on.

2. For an example of a poem written in iambic pentameter—five iambs per line—look at An Essay on Man by Alexander Pope.

Answers

1. The number of feet in a line determines the meter; trimeter is written in three-foot lines, tetrameter in four-foot lines, and so on.

2. For an example of a poem written in iambic pentameter—five iambs per line—look at "An Essay on Man" by Alexander Pope.

Day 5

Skills Practiced

Use of dashes to set off interrupter that already contains commas

Subject and verb agreement

Elimination of double negative

Use of semicolon and comma with a conjunctive adverb to correct run-on sentence

Correction of commonly confused words

Practice Sentences

1. Common measure, the popular meter found in ballads, hymns, nursery rhymes, and cheers, alternate four-foot and three-foot lines.

2. The rhythm of hardly no poems fits a meter exactly, indeed departure from the meter is often a way to achieve a poetic affect.

Answers

1. Common measure—the popular meter found in many ballads, hymns, nursery rhymes, and cheers—alternates four-foot and three-foot lines.

2. The rhythm of hardly any poems fits a meter exactly; indeed, departure from the meter is often a way to achieve a poetic effect.

Day 1

Skills Practiced

Correction of commonly misspelled word

Correction of misplaced participle

Use of vivid verb to improve style

Elimination of redundancy

Revision of a sentence ending with a preposition

Practice Sentences

1. Virginia Woolf pioneered the stream of conciousness technique, using characters' feelings, memories, and thoughts.

2. The random flow of thoughts through a character's mind is what Woolf's fiction and novels are all about.

Answers

1. Using characters' feelings, memories, and thoughts, Virginia Woolf pioneered the narrative technique called stream of consciousness.

2. Woolf's fiction depicts the random flow of thoughts through a character's mind.

Day 2

Skills Practiced

Use of hyphens with compound adjective

Use of comma after introductory phrase

Use of commas in a series

Use of commas to set off adjectives following noun

Practice Sentences

1. When reading a stream of consciousness narrative the reader must organize a meaningful whole from the intermingled thoughts memories and dialogue.

2. This task demanding and rewarding reveals an intense and psychologically complete portrait of a character.

Answers

1. When reading a stream-of-consciousness narrative, the reader must organize a meaningful whole from the intermingled thoughts, memories, and dialogue.

2. This task, demanding and rewarding, reveals an intense and psychologically complete portrait of a character.

Day 3

Skills Practiced

Revision of wordy sentence

Elimination of superlative form of absolute adjective

Use of adverb to modify verb

Elimination of unnecessary exclamation point

Practice Sentences

1. Katherine Mansfield was an innovative writer on account of the fact that she focused on characters' most innermost states and heightened awareness.

2. Even when little happens outward, her story dialogue reveals complex moods and conflicts!

Answers

1. Katherine Mansfield was an innovative writer in that she focused on characters' innermost states and heightened awareness.

2. Even when little happens outwardly, her story dialogue reveals complex moods and conflicts.

Day 4

Skills Practiced

Subject and verb agreement

Use of commas in a series

Elimination of redundancy

Correct pronoun case after *than*

Correct spelling of homophones

Practice Sentences

1. The powerful novels of Doris Lessing explores the evils of racism the role of women in society and the complexities of today's modern-day life.

2. Few contemporary novels are more distinguished than them for there breadth of vision.

Answers

1. The powerful novels of Doris Lessing explore the evils of racism, the role of women in society, and the complexities of modern-day life.

2. Few contemporary novels are more distinguished than they for their breadth of vision.

Day 5

Skills Practiced

Streamlining sentence with possessive form

Correct use of colon before a list

Revision of choppy sentences

Practice Sentences

1. The protagonists of the novels of Margaret Drabble are frequently well-educated professional women, scholars, poets, journalists.

2. They are often faced with the dilemma of integrating family life and careers. They break with tradition. They chart new lifestyles and patterns of living.

Answers

1. The protagonists of Margaret Drabble's novels are frequently well-educated professional women: scholars, poets, journalists.

2. Often faced with the dilemma of integrating family life and careers, they break with tradition and chart new lifestyles and patterns of living.

Daily Language Practice • Week 31

Day 1

Skills Practiced

Addition of adjective qualifier

Capitalization of name of award

Spelling out ordinal numbers

Use of possessive pronoun before gerund

Correct past form of irregular verb

Practice Sentences

1. Critics consider William Butler Yeats, the winner of the 1923 nobel prize for literature, to be the finest lyric poet of the 20th century.

2. Yeats's interest in Irish folklore and history led to him joining the Irish National Movement, whose members seeked Ireland's independence from Britain.

Answers

1. Many critics consider William Butler Yeats, the winner of the 1923 Nobel Prize for Literature, to be the finest lyric poet of the twentieth century.

2. Yeats's interest in Irish folklore and history led to his joining the Irish National Movement, whose members sought Ireland's independence from Britain.

Day 2

Skills Practiced

Use of comma before coordinating conjunction in compound sentence

Use of adverb to modify adjective

Use of quotation marks with title of a poem

Elimination of *you* without a clear antecedent

Use of helping verb *have*

Practice Sentences

1. Yeats once planned to become an artist like his father and his early poems were dreamy pictorial, suggesting lovely landscapes lit by twilight.

2. The Lake Isle of Innisfree is from this period, and in it you sense the mystical enchantment that the Irish countryside must of inspired in the young poet.

Answers

1. Yeats once planned to become an artist like his father, and his early poems were dreamily pictorial, suggesting lovely landscapes lit by twilight.

2. "The Lake Isle of Innisfree" is from this period, and in it readers sense the mystical enchantment that the Irish countryside must have inspired in the young poet.

Day 3

Skills Practiced

Revision of choppy sentences

Elimination of double comparison

Subject and verb agreement

Elimination of faulty parallel structure

Practice Sentences

1. Yeats was essentially a poet and mystic. He believed that truth is reached through beauty. He believed that imagination is more stronger than reason.

2. The haunting quality of his best poems result from the clarity of their imagery and their being musical.

Answers

1. Essentially a poet and mystic, Yeats believed that truth is reached through beauty and that imagination is stronger than reason.

2. The haunting quality of his best poems results from the clarity of their imagery and their music.

Day 4

Skills Practiced

Use of past perfect tense

Correction of commonly confused words

Use of commas to set off parallel element

Subject and verb agreement

Practice Sentences

1. In later years, as Yeats tired of the romantic enchantments that thrilled him as a young man, he adapted a plainer style.

2. Irish nationalism particularly Yeats's desire for a popular style to express Irish aspirations were also responsible for this change.

Answers

1. In later years, as Yeats tired of the romantic enchantments that had thrilled him as a young man, he adopted a plainer style.

2. Irish nationalism, particularly Yeats's desire for a popular style to express Irish aspirations, was also responsible for this change.

Day 5

Skills Practiced

Use of commas with interrupters

Correction of unclear pronoun reference

Use of exclamation mark to show strong emotion

Subject and verb agreement

Spelling out numerals for decades

Practice Sentences

1. How extraordinary that Yeats's poetry unlike so many others actually improved as he aged.

2. Much of his best work including "The Second Coming" and "Sailing to Byzantium" were written when he was in his 60's and 70's.

Answers

1. How extraordinary that Yeats's poetry, unlike the work of so many other poets, improved as he aged!

2. Much of his best work, including "The Second Coming" and "Sailing to Byzantium," was written when he was in his sixties and seventies.

Daily Language Practice • Week 32

Day 1

Skills Practiced

Correction of misplaced modifier

Verb tense compatibility

Revision of stringy sentence

Correct pronoun case

Practice Sentences

1. Pygmalion gradually falls in love with a statue of a woman that he was sculpting in Greek legend.

2. Aphrodite grants Pygmalion's wish because she is the goddess of love, and she made the statue become a living woman who the sculptor then marries.

Answers

1. In Greek legend, Pygmalion gradually falls in love with a statue of a woman that he is sculpting.

2. Aphrodite, the goddess of love, grants Pygmalion's wish and makes the statue become a living woman whom the sculptor then marries.

Day 2

Skills Practiced

Use of italics or underlining for title of play

Revision of sentence ending with a preposition

Correct use of indefinite article

Use of quotation marks to call attention to specific words and phrases

Use of adverb to modify verb

Practice Sentences

1. George Bernard Shaw's play Pygmalion is a modern retelling of the Greek myth it is named for.

2. The play recounts how an ignorant girl becomes a elegant lady in Cinderella-like fashion; her fairy godmother, however, is an Englishman who teaches her to speak and act correct.

Answers

1. George Bernard Shaw's play <u>Pygmalion</u> is a modern retelling of the Greek myth for which it is named.

2. The play recounts how an ignorant girl becomes an elegant lady in Cinderella-like fashion; her "fairy godmother," however, is an Englishman who teaches her to speak and act correctly.

Day 3

Skills Practiced

Correction of commonly misspelled word

Elimination of faulty parallel structure

Elimination of *but* after *help*

Use of commas in a series

Practice Sentences

1. George Bernard Shaw was both a playright and wanted to reform society; in his plays he couldn't help but treat serious social issues.

2. <u>Pygmalion</u> is an attack on England's class system; in other plays, Shaw criticized slumlords war profiteers and the inequities of the industrial system.

Answers

1. George Bernard Shaw was both a playwright and social reformer; in his plays he couldn't help treating serious social issues.

2. <u>Pygmalion</u> is an attack on England's class system; in other plays, Shaw criticized slumlords, war profiteers, and the inequities of the industrial system.

Day 4

Skills Practiced

Use of active voice to improve style

Use of semicolon between main clauses to correct run-on sentences

Use of underlining or italics with title of long musical work

Practice Sentences

1. Poor flowergirl Eliza Doolittle is transformed into a counterfeit aristocrat and demonstrates the absurdity of class distinctions.

2. <u>Pygmalion</u> has proved to be Shaw's most successful work, the play inspired a popular movie and the musical "My Fair Lady."

Answers

1. Eliza Doolittle's transformation from a poor flowergirl into a counterfeit aristocrat demonstrates the absurdity of class distinctions.

2. <u>Pygmalion</u> has proved to be Shaw's most successful work; the play inspired a popular movie and the musical <u>My Fair Lady</u>.

Day 5

Skills Practiced

Correct capitalization and punctuation of sentence in parentheses

Spelling out numbers through one hundred

Correct use of commas with a split quotation

Use of quotation marks in a split quotation

Practice Sentences

1. During his long life (He lived to be ninety-four.) and in more than 50 plays, Shaw tried to shake his audiences out of their complacencies and hypocrisies.

2. "I must warn my readers Shaw once wrote that my attacks are directed against themselves, not against my stage characters."

Answers

1. During his long life (he lived to be ninety-four) and in more than fifty plays, Shaw tried to shake his audiences out of their complacencies and hypocrisies.

2. "I must warn my readers," Shaw once wrote, "that my attacks are directed against themselves, not against my stage characters."

Daily Language Practice • Week 33

Day 1

Skills Practiced

Correct use of prepositions *between* and *among*

Use of conjunctive adverb

Elimination of comma in compound predicate

Practice Sentences

1. Long-standing tensions existed between the nations of Europe so in 1914 World War I erupted.

2. The bloody conflict decimated an entire generation of young men, and shredded the fabric of British society.

Answers

1. Long-standing tensions existed among the nations of Europe; as a result, in 1914 World War I erupted.

2. The bloody conflict decimated an entire generation of young men and shredded the fabric of British society.

Day 2

Skills Practiced

Correct relative pronoun

Use of end punctuation: question mark

Correction of commonly confused words

Correct past form of irregular verb

Practice Sentences

1. What caused this vast slaughter which pitted the Allies, including the British Empire and France, against the Central Powers of Germany and Austria-Hungary.

2. Beside the rise of nationalism and competition for colonies, widespread military alliances created an atmosphere in which hostilities become inevitable.

Answers

1. What caused this vast slaughter that pitted the Allies, including the British Empire and France, against the Central Powers of Germany and Austria-Hungary?

2. Besides the rise of nationalism and competition for colonies, widespread military alliances created an atmosphere in which hostilities became inevitable.

Day 3

Skills Practiced	Practice Sentences
Use of verb in the subjunctive mood Correction of commonly confused words Correct spelling: doubling final consonant Elimination of faulty parallel structure Correct use of periods with parentheses	1. As if the fighting in France was not enough, the British military was challenged farther in 1916 when nationalists in Ireland rebeled. 2. The great upsurge in Irish nationalism led to independence in 1921 and creating the Irish Free State (now the Republic of Ireland.) **Answers** 1. As if the fighting in France were not enough, the British military was challenged further in 1916 when nationalists in Ireland rebeled. 2. The great upsurge in Irish nationalism led to independence in 1921 and the creation of the Irish Free State (now the Republic of Ireland).

Day 4

Skills Practiced	Practice Sentences
Capitalization of name of document Verb tense compatibility Inclusion of closing quotation marks Elimination of double comparison Elimination of question mark with indirect question	1. When the armistice was signed in 1918, all Europe is exhausted by what the British once called "the Great War for Civilization. 2. Hard times after the war led to worser despair, and there is little reason to ask why the youth of postwar Europe was called a "lost generation"? **Answers** 1. When the Armistice was signed in 1918, all Europe was exhausted by what the British once called "the Great War for Civilization." 2. Hard times after the war led to worse despair, and there is little reason to ask why the youth of postwar Europe was called a "lost generation."

Day 5

Skills Practiced	Practice Sentences
Correction of unclear pronoun reference Correct past form of irregular verb Use of comma to indicate omitted but understood words in a parallel construction Correct relative pronoun	1. After the war, many Europeans were destitute and jobless, which made political extremes more attractive. 2. In Italy and Germany, fascist dictators arised, and in Russia communists, that cast shadows over the continent's future. **Answers** 1. After the war, many Europeans were destitute and jobless, and they found political extremes more attractive. 2. In Italy and Germany, fascist dictators arose, and in Russia, communists, who cast shadows over the continent's future.

Daily Language Practice • Week 34

Day 1

Skills Practiced

Use of comma to set off appositive

Use of periods with initials

Correction of faulty subordination

Elimination of comma in compound predicate

Practice Sentences

1. A poet, playwright, and critic T S Eliot was a major influence in the reshaping of modern literature after World War I.

2. Because it is often difficult to understand, Eliot's poetry draws upon, and makes allusions to history, myth, foreign languages, and religion.

Answers

1. A poet, playwright, and critic, T. S. Eliot was a major influence in the reshaping of modern literature after World War I.

2. Because Eliot's poetry draws upon and makes allusions to history, myth, foreign languages, and religion, it is often difficult to understand.

Day 2

Skills Practiced

Elimination of unnecessary prepositions

Elimination of commas with restrictive appositive

Use of hyphen with the prefix *post-*

Use of adverb to modify an adjective

Use of predicate adjective after linking verb

Practice Sentences

1. T. S. Eliot believed that modern culture was decaying badly, and his early poetry, up until around the middle of the 1920's, explored this theme.

2. As his masterpiece, <u>The Waste Land</u>, makes clear, conditions in post World War I Europe looked real badly when contrasted with earlier times.

Answers

1. T. S. Eliot believed that modern culture was decaying badly, and his early poetry, until the middle of the 1920's, explored this theme.

2. As his masterpiece <u>The Waste Land</u> makes clear, conditions in post-World War I Europe looked really bad when contrasted with earlier times.

	Skills Practiced	Practice Sentences
Day 3	Correction of commonly misspelled word Correct capitalization in titles Subject and verb agreement Elimination of double subject	1. In tone and mood, Eliot's later poetry, such as "Ash Wensday" and "Journey Of The Magi," are more hopeful. 2. This later work, including Eliot's last major poem, <u>Four Quartets</u>, a meditation on time and timelessness, it reflects the poet's religious feelings. **Answers** 1. In tone and mood, Eliot's later poetry, such as "Ash Wednesday" and "Journey of the Magi," is more hopeful. 2. This later work, including Eliot's last major poem, <u>Four Quartets</u>, a meditation on time and timelessness, reflects the poet's religious feelings.

	Skills Practiced	Practice Sentences
Day 4	Correct use of *fewer* and *less* Use of active voice to improve style Correct past participle of irregular verb Pronoun agreement with antecedent	1. In later years, Eliot wrote less poems; instead, his attention was turned to writing poetic dramas. 2. He wrote these plays in verse that is so conversational that when spoke in the theater, they do not sound like verse at all. **Answers** 1. In later years, Eliot wrote fewer poems; instead, he turned his attention to writing poetic dramas. 2. He wrote these plays in verse that is so conversational that when spoken in the theater, it does not sound like verse at all.

	Skills Practiced	Practice Sentences
Day 5	Use of hyphen with compound adjective Use of commas with non-restrictive clause Use of adverb Use of comma after introductory phrase Use of underlining or italics with title of long musical work	1. The Missouri born Eliot who became a British subject in 1927 received the Nobel Prize for Literature in 1948. 2. Surprising enough the popular musical Cats was based on a collection of T. S. Eliot's poems about his favorite cats. **Answers** 1. The Missouri-born Eliot, who became a British subject in 1927, received the Nobel Prize for Literature in 1948. 2. Surprisingly enough, the popular musical <u>Cats</u> was based on a collection of T. S. Eliot's poems about his favorite cats.

Day 1

Skills Practiced

Spelling out ordinal numbers

Use of present perfect tense

Use of verb in the subjunctive mood

Capitalization of name of historical period

Elimination of split infinitive

Practice Sentences

1. From the late 19th century to the present day, artists veered away from using traditional concepts and techniques in painting.

2. As if art was suddenly freed from traditions stretching back to the renaissance, artists began to truly delight in freer brushwork and colors.

Answers

1. From the late nineteenth century to the present day, artists have veered away from using traditional concepts and techniques in painting.

2. As if art were suddenly freed from traditions stretching back to the Renaissance, artists truly began to delight in freer brushwork and colors.

Day 2

Skills Practiced

Correction of faulty parallel structure

Correction of commonly confused words

Correction of unclear pronoun reference

Use of dashes to emphasize additional information

Elimination of double negative

Practice Sentences

1. Changes in style and using new techniques, which allowed artists to express new ideas, created a separation between the subject of a painting and it's image.

2. As they became more independent and subjective in their views, officials of the church and state—once their main patrons, couldn't hardly continue to support artists.

Answers

1. Changes in style and techniques, which allowed artists to express new ideas, created a separation between the subject of a painting and its image.

2. As artists became more independent and subjective in their views, officials of the church and state—once the artists' main patrons—couldn't continue to support them.

Day 3

Skills Practiced

Use of comma before coordinating conjunction in a compound sentence

Correction of misplaced modifier

Elimination of empty sentence

Practice Sentences

1. Flouting the laws of perspective, some artists extracted geometrical forms from nature; or they created radically new spatial relationships.

2. The pure and simplified shapes of primitive art in the early twentieth century also inspired artists. This was a real inspiration.

Answers

1. Flouting the laws of perspective, some artists extracted geometrical forms from nature, or they created radically new spatial relationships.

2. The pure and simplified shapes of primitive art also inspired artists in the early twentieth century.

Day 4

Skills Practiced

Use of adverb to modify adjective

Correction of commonly confused words

Elimination of superlative form with absolute adjective

Correction of commonly misspelled word

Practice Sentences

1. As time passed, painters increasingly emphasized pure visual impact rather then recognizable subject matter.

2. Color reigned most supreme and was soon transformed into an abstract art completely seperated from subject matter.

Answers

1. As time passed, painters increasingly emphasized purely visual impact rather than recognizable subject matter.

2. Color reigned supreme and was soon transformed into an abstract art completely separated from subject matter.

Day 5

Skills Practiced

Elimination of redundancy

Use of correct form of reflexive pronoun

Revision of sentence ending with a preposition

Use of semicolon and comma with a conjunctive adverb to correct run-on sentence

Use of comma after introductory clause

Practice Sentences

1. Many countless movements have risen in modern art, each offering new styles and techniques for artists to express theirselves with.

2. The public often greets each new phase of modern art with ridicule however as the shock wears off the movement influences and inspires new artists.

Answers

1. Countless movements have risen in modern art, each offering new styles and techniques with which artists express themselves.

2. The public often greets each new phase of modern art with ridicule; however, as the shock wears off, the movement influences and inspires new artists.

Day 1

Skills Practiced

Correct pronoun case

Use of comma in a series

Use of quotation marks to call attention to specific word

Practice Sentences

1. Have you ever wondered how some people, who we call creative geniuses, are able to express themselves in marvelous and original ways?

2. We might ascribe a great painting poem or piece of music to an artist's genius; this term, however, doesn't say anything about the source of creativity.

Answers

1. Have you ever wondered how some people, whom we call creative geniuses, are able to express themselves in marvelous and original ways?

2. We might ascribe a great painting, poem, or piece of music to an artist's "genius"; this term, however, doesn't say anything about the source of creativity.

Day 2

Skills Practiced

Use of semicolon between main clauses to correct run-on sentence

Correction of unclear pronoun reference

Correct relative pronoun

Practice Sentences

1. Some writers claim that their best stories and poems simply "came" to them, they were mere instruments to record the inspiration.

2. Similarly, composers as great as Mozart and Beethoven were attuned to some celestial music which suggested themes for concerti and symphonies.

Answers

1. Some writers claim that their best stories and poems simply "came" to them; these writers were mere instruments to record the inspiration.

2. Similarly, composers as great as Mozart and Beethoven were attuned to some celestial music that suggested themes for concerti and symphonies.

Day 3

Skills Practiced

Elimination of modifier with absolute adjective

Use of commas with interrupter

Use of quotation marks with title of a poem

Elimination of *and* at the beginning of a sentence

Elimination of unnecessary comma between subject and verb

Practice Sentences

1. Dreams supplied many artists with very unique imagery and sometimes as in the case of Samuel Taylor Coleridge's Kubla Khan the actual text of a poem.

2. And dreaming about dancing carbon atoms, led Friedrich Kekulé to major discoveries about the structure of molecules.

Answers

1. Dreams supplied many artists with unique imagery and sometimes, as in the case of Samuel Taylor Coleridge's "Kubla Khan," the actual text of a poem.

2. Dreaming about dancing carbon atoms led Friedrich Kekulé to major discoveries about the structure of molecules.

Day 4

Skills Practiced

Elimination of hyphen in closed compound noun

Subject and verb agreement

Use of quotation marks to show a speaker's exact words in a split quotation

Practice Sentences

1. The art-work of Jackson Pollock, who went into a trance to paint, support the view that creativity is often not conscious work.

2. "When I am in my painting, Pollock once noted, I am not aware of what I am doing... the painting has a life of its own."

Answers

1. The artwork of Jackson Pollock, who went into a trance to paint, supports the view that creativity is often not conscious work.

2. "When I am in my painting," Pollock once noted, "I am not aware of what I am doing . . . the painting has a life of its own."

Day 5

Skills Practiced

Correction of misplaced modifier

Correction of commonly confused words

Subject and verb agreement

Use of hyphen with the prefix *all-*

Elimination of faulty parallel structure

Practice Sentences

1. Whether there aware of it or not, the cultural legacy—myths, folklore, and art—are all important to artists, and we see them return to it frequently.

2. Vitalizing, shaping, and to refine the raw material that the mind provides—this too is the work of creativity.

Answers

1. The cultural legacy—myths, folklore, and art—is all-important to artists, and we see them return to it frequently, whether they're aware of it or not.

2. Vitalizing, shaping, and refining the raw material that the mind provides—this too is the work of creativity.